THE
RELENTLESS
PURSUIT OF A
SOUL

CARL MILLER

Published in the United States of America

Brilliant Books Literary
137 Forest Park Lane Thomasville
North Carolina 27360 USA

ISBN:
Paperback: 979-8-88945-511-0
Ebook: 979-8-88945-512-7

LAYING THE FOUNDATION

ON A COLD DECEMBER NIGHT IN Marshall, Texas, a young woman full of both fear and anticipation is suddenly overcome by an intense pain. Not a bad pain. This is a pain that is associated with new life, her son's life. Oh, how she has longed for this moment. Oh, how she has prayed for his safe arrival.

At the first pang and with the dawning realization of what it portends, she bows her head and prays. "Heavenly Father, I humbly come before You, asking for Your grace and protection over my first-born son. Father, I dedicate my son to you. I ask only, Father, that if he will not come to know the Salvation from You, through Your Son, Jesus, that You will call him home now. Lord, I love my son, but I would rather never to have known him than to have him, lovingly watch him grow, and then see him die separated from You. Father, if it is Your will for me to have this child, please send Your Spirit to guide me in the direction that leads him to You."

When her prayer ended, the next labor pain started. The feeling of anticipation returned. Much to her relief, she now felt a sense of excitement instead of fear accompanying that anticipation. Approximately twenty hours later, she was introduced to her new son. "Hello, Carl," she said. "Your father and I have been waiting for you."

A photograph of young Carl topped the birth announcement stating that Chris and Rhonda Miller were the proud parents of this 9 pound, 10 ounce boy measuring 22.5 inches long, who came into this world on December 9, 1969.

"Praise be to You, Lord," Chris prayed. "Thank you for my son." Chris was a young, hopeful Christian evangelist who was finishing up seminary in East Texas. He was in agreement with Rhonda on the dedication of their son to the Lord. Because of the call to minister that Chris felt upon his life, accompanied by the strong Christian devotion from his wife and both sets of their parents, young Carl's future walk with the Lord seemed almost set in stone. Just as God the Father,who created and loves us, reigns in heaven, the enemy, commonly known as Satan, roams the earth like a roaring lion, seeking whom he may devour.

———— • ◆ • ————

A smirk emerged on Kansra's face as he witnessed young Carl's parents lovingly dedicate their son to God. A high ranking soldier demon, he was assigned to monitor the arrival of all new souls to the central and eastern Texas regions. His responsibilities included gathering various bits of information about each new child and compiling a detailed report for his master. The report contained detailed facts about the child's health, his or her parents' health, the marital relationship of the parents, and most importantly—whether there is any substantiated belief that Jesus Christ is the Son of the Most High God. Kansra assessed each case and assigned a personal demon to each new soul.

Kansra let his sly gaze slide around the room. His master would appear soon. Satan especially took interest in the arrival of a new child to the parents that are followers of Christ.

"Hello Kansra," Satan said as he suddenly appeared. "I see we have another set of hopeful fools who think they can decide their child's path in life."

"Yes, sire," replied Kansra. "This boy is the latest challenge to arrive this week."

Satan's gaze turned from the boy to Kansra. "That's part of the reason I'm here. Do you have enough personnel?"

"Well, sire, all of my veteran tempters are handling multiple challenges, so I've decided to promote a few worthy candidates. For this boy, I plan to use a new eager tempter named Nakot."

"Nakot, huh," replied Satan, "Why him?"

Kansra cleared his throat as he started to answer, "Well, sire, Nakot has shown a great deal of potential in the last few decades. He is currently on assignment in the eastern region of the African continent. I promoted him from tormentor of the damned to a tempter of the living at the beginning of the Second World War. He seemed eager enough, and his daily tally of souls was impressive."

"Well of course it was," chuckled Satan as he turned his gaze back to the new child. "Anyone of my legionnaires can tally souls in a time of war. I don't doubt Nakot's tempting skills proved impressive when used on the Nazi regime. I do, however, question your judgment about his skills when faced with a challenging case. I mean, that boy doesn't have just one parent praying for him.

He has both parents, both sets of grandparents, and even his aunts and uncles are born-again followers of Christ who have been and will continue praying for him.

Are you sure Nakot is ready for that kind of challenge?"

I sure hope so, ran through Kansra's head as he looked Satan in the eye. He confidently said, "Yes, sire, I know he can do it."

There was an uncomfortable pause of silence as Satan turned his stare to Kansra. "I hope for your sake that you're right. You should know, I'll be checking in from time to time on this case."

"Yes, sire. I'll look forward to seeing you."

Satan cracked a sarcastic smile. "I'm sure you will."

Satan vanished in a cloud of mist. Kansra stood contemplating what Satan said. He knew if he appointed Nakot, then Nakot better be able to handle the job. "Tempters are not always successful, he knows that," Kansra mumbled to himself. "Why then would he question me about Nakot?"

Suddenly it occurred to him that this would be his first promotion of a new tempter to a challenging case. I wonder, he thought to himself, *Did Lucifer himself promote these other veteran tempters or were they promoted by former captains who no longer hold that rank? If Nakot fails, will I lose my rank?* Kansra shook his head as he pondered his own questions. "Well, he said to himself, "I'll just have to make sure Nakot doesn't fail."

Kansra turned around to find Satan had reappeared and was standing directly behind him. "Sire!" Kansra exclaimed with nervous excitement. "What brings you back so soon?"

Again Satan displayed a sarcastic smirk, "Something troubling you, Kansra?"

Kansra straightened out of his cringing crouch into perfect posture. "No, sire, I-I was just going over some logistics for my battle plans."

"Ahh," Satan appraised him, his smirk still in place. "Well, I almost forgot the second reason I came to see you today. I have assembled a small team to accompany me to Southeast Asia. I want you to be part of that team. My bounty of souls grows each day this new war rages between the Americans and the North Vietnamese."

Kansra bowed his head. "You honor me, sire, thank you. When do we leave?"

"I'll come for you in a week. That should give you enough time to get things lined up around here." Again, before Kansra could comment, Satan vanished.

"A week," Kansra said, his voice week with disbelief. "How am I supposed to assign a challenge to a new tempter and properly train him in a week? It's almost as if I'm being set up to fail." Kansra shook his head violently as if to shake off any feelings of worry. "Let's go find Nakot," he said to himself as he departed from East Texas. In the blink of an eye, Kansra appeared on a barren plain. The only thing that broke the hazy horizon was the juvenile militants circling their prey.

"Come on now, you know you can't let that child live. That child is evil. She is not from your tribe. If you allow her to live, she'll raise sons that will one day rape your daughters. Kill her quick and there will be no worries. Come on now, do it. Do it!" ordered Nakot as he circled round a young militant.

Kansra hovered over Nakot for a moment to watch him work.

"Come on now, kill her, do it, you know you must do it," repeated Nakot into the ear of the young rebel fighter. Nakot seemed crazed as he chanted it over and over, "Kill her, kill her," until a loud shot rang out across the plains.

"Hah!" Nakot exclaimed before snuggling up to the soldier and whisperingin his ear, "You did the right thing. Now, let's go have a drink, you deserve one."

Nakot threw his arms out wide as he laughed and bragged to the air about his lethal skills. He started to dance, and in the middle of a spin he saw Kansra standing there watching him.

"Kansra", he said with embarrassment and surprise. He recovered his bravado quickly. "Did you see that? Did you see what I just did? I got skills, huh?" "Not bad, Nakot," remarked Kansra. "You definitely seem to be enjoying yourself."

"Oh yes, sir," replied Nakot. "I'm loving this tempting stuff. It's so much more rewarding than tormenting the damned."

"Good, because you're going to need that level of enthusiasm for your next assignment."

Nakot perked up, his pumpkin-shaped head rolling precariously on his shoulders. "What is it? Do I finally get a challenging case, do I, do I?"

"Slow down Nakot," barked Kansra. "Stop acting like an idiot and let me talk. Yes, you are going to have your first challenging case. I'm assigning you to a new child in America."

Finally, Nakot thought. *It's about time they recognize me for the skills I got.*

"Nakot!" Kansra yelled. "Are you listening to me?" "Yes, sire, of course I am!" Nakot bowed repeatedly.

Kansra paused for a moment to study Nakot. He started getting the feeling that maybe he was making a mistake with Nakot. *Well*, Kansra thought, *if I don't use Nakot, then who will I use? Yeah, it'll be all right, he'll do fine.*

Kansra turned away from Nakot as he said, "Come, Nakot. I'll take you to your new assignment."

Kansra and Nakot came to an abrupt stop in the parking lot of the hospital. Nakot circled around the empty lot searching for his new case. "Where is it, sire, where's my new challenge, huh, where is it?"

Kansra's patience was gone. "Shut up you fool. You are making me doubt my decision to promote you."

Nakot came to an abrupt stop, slouched, and lowered his head, like that of a child being scolded by his parent.

Kansra regained his composure and began to speak, "Before we go inside the hospital, I want to give you some direction. I'm assigning you to a newborn son. For the next several years, you are to do nothing more than observe Dakkas.

Dakkas has been working on the child's parents for years now. Dakkas is a pro. You would be wise to learn all you can from him. Until the child is of age ten, you are to work with Dakkas under his command. You are to assist him in tempting the parents."

"Yes, sir, sire," replied Nakot. "With both me and Dakkas on them, they don't stand a chance."

Kansra shook his head. "Oh, Nakot, your eagerness outweighs your abilities.

These are nothing like the souls you've tempted in the past. The child's parents are both born-again followers of Christ. We stand no chance of claiming their souls. The reason Dakkas works them so diligently is to divide them. You see, if we can divide the parents, then we stand a much better chance with the child. The child's soul is fair game. Just because the parents are safe, doesn't mean the child will be. I can't over-emphasize the importance of destroying the marital relationship of the parents. Destroying the home has been one of our greatest weapons in this war. If you succeed with that, then the boy will be much more susceptible to your taunts. Remember, you must be relentless in your pursuit of this soul."

"Yes, sir, sire," replied Nakot. "I'll have him in no time."

Have you heard nothing I said, thought Kansra as he stared emotionless at Nakot. "Well, for your sake, I hope you're right."

"Oh, I'm right, sire, you'll see," replied Nakot. "When can I expect to see you again?"

Kansra hesitated, trying to decide if he wanted to tell him anything. "I don't know," Kansra said, "I'm accompanying Lucifer to the other side of the earth. He selected me to assist him with the war taking place in Asia. If all goes well, you won't see me again for several years."

"Wow," said Nakot, "maybe one day I'll be assisting Lucifer on a mission."

Yeah right! Kansra thought to himself as he laughed and said, "Maybe one day, but first, let's see how you do with this case. Now, go inside and get with Dakkas. He'll line you out and get you started. I'll be back when the war is over. I'll expect a good report from you when I return. Do I make myself clear?"

Nakot quickly replied, "Yes, sire, I will not fail you.

———— ◆ ◆◆ ◆ ————

Six years passed, the Vietnam War ended, and as promised, Kansra returned for a full report from all of his soldiers. "Dakkas, I'd like a detailed summary of where you and Nakot are with the Millers."

Before Dakkas could respond, Nakot chimed in, "Well, sire, after four years of relentless influence, we were able to convince Chris, the child's father, that life as an evangelist was not his true calling. We convinced him that he would prosper more as the owner of a small contractor business."

"Did he take the bait?" asked Kansra.

"Yes, sire, he no longer preaches the message of Christ. His marriage is riddled with strife, and I have personally seen to the influence of adultery."

"How is he responding to your influence?"

"Very well, Master. I believe it will not be much longer before he succumbs to the will of his flesh."

"Excellent!" roared Kansra. "Every one of the souls we collect from those pathetic humans brings me joy, but I am especially fond of destroying the lives of those who choose to follow the path of Christ. Stay relentless with your influence.

If you can destroy that family you'll have a better chance of laying a good foundation with the child."

"Yes, sire," responded Nakot. "I'll get him".

Eventually, Nakot's spirit of adultery overwhelmed Chris. Overcome by the lust for another woman, Chris made a decision that changed the lives of his entire family.

THE VICES START TURNING

MY PARENTS' SEMI-SHORT MARRIAGE ending abruptly through an ugly divorce is a common story for many families today. Here in America, nearly half of all marriages end in divorce. I don't know if my parents' separation had any influence on the path I chose for my life. I only know that for some reason, all throughout my life, I was plagued by a sense of inadequacy. I believe the feeling of inadequacy paved the road that I so earnestly followed.

I was fortunate enough to have a caring mother who saw to it that I was raised to know about Jesus. Of course, as a young person, I did not appreciate her efforts. As a result of my parents' divorce, I moved around a lot from the second through the eighth grade. Kids at those ages are oftentimes very mean—especially to the new kids in school. Every new school in every new town meant attending a new church. Kids are Kids. Oftentimes, they are just as mean in the church as they are in school.

Looking back on it now, I realize that it wasn't so much the kids being mean to me as much as it was me being afraid of everything. Apparently, the feelings of fear follow the feelings of inadequacy.

In the eighth grade, I started drinking beer with my older cousin's boyfriend. I didn't like the taste, but I really liked the way it made me feel. I realized that after a few Miller Light ponies, all of the feelings of inadequacy and fear left me. I suddenly felt bold, confident and better looking. Alcohol has a funny way of doing that to people. The term *beer goggles* implies that when someone's drunk, a person from the opposite sex, despite their features, is suddenly very attractive. *Beer goggles* can also mean that a person cannot see the effects that alcohol has on their life.

I had on beer goggles. I never did drink right. I drank to get drunk as often as I could. Life without fear is glorious, indeed. The problem with using something like alcohol to overcome problematic feelings in your life is that it often becomes a vice. Without the alcohol, I was an uncool, scared teenager. No one wants to be uncool. No one wants to be scared.

Between the eighth and ninth grade I moved from my mother's house to my father's. My mother, brother, and I had moved back to the same small town my father lived in at the beginning of my eighth grade year. Most of the kids I went to school with were the same kids I had gone to school with until the second grade. I enjoyed the popularity I felt from being the kid who came back from living abroad. There was only one thing I thought I needed to increase my popularity—money. My mother didn't have much. We lived in an old mobile home, and she drove an old car. My father, on the other hand, was doing quite well with his business. He had a nice brick home, in a nice neighborhood, with nice new vehicles sitting in the driveway. It pains me to think that I broke my mother's heart by moving out for reasons so shallow, but that's what I did.

I joined the golf team my ninth grade year. I was getting drunk three to four times a week with whatever types of alcohol I could get my hands on. I had to go to church with my family, but the message the church was preaching went against everything I thought was cool. I wanted to listen to the hardest death metal I could find. I would fantasize about how cool it would be to start a band and call it Dark Angel. The only problem I could see with that dream was that I could not sing or play and type of musical instrument. I now am thankful that I possess no music skills, or I might not be here telling this story.

In addition to the alcohol, I started smoking pot my ninth grade year. I wasn't real fond of the high that accompanied pot. Oftentimes, after just a few hits, I felt too high. I didn't like the feeling that I was not in control. With alcohol, I could regulate—after just a few drinks—how many I needed to consume to keep me at the "ideal buzz" level.

With pot, it was a roll of the dice—some weed was stronger than others. I remember thinking that I must be some type of wimp. My buddies always wanted to smoke a whole fat joint, where I only wanted to take one or two light hits. Of course, at age fourteen, being a wimp is out of the question. I quickly learned how to take dummy hits. I would go through all the motions of a real hit, but I wouldn't inhale. I would still get a little high from holding the smoke in my mouth and throat for so long, but that's exactly what I was looking for—a little high.

From an early age, I learned that the best way to protect my ability to drink and use was to conceal it. As you can imagine, drinking and drugging as a teenager living in a Christian home created certain problems for me and the lifestyle I wanted to live. As I mentioned before, church was a requirement. Some of my friends from school attended the same church I attended. At the time, this church was probably the largest within the county that I was living in. During the summers, we had one hundred plus members in the youth group.

Being not just popular, but the most popular guy was an achievement I diligently strove for. Looking back, I now realize that I was pretty popular. My picture went into the high school yearbook as Freshman Class Favorite. I played football and golf, though I was not spectacular at either one. I remember thinking that if I was better at these sports, then I would be as popular as I wanted to be. I mean, why couldn't I be the cool quarterback or the guy shooting just above par in the golf tournaments? A feeling of inadequacy can be much like the feelings of anorexia. Instead of seeing myself as fat, I saw myself as a scared "wanna-be" instead of the good natured kid I truly was. Of course, as any alcoholic can tell you, when in doubt, drink. When I drank, all of those inferiority feelings were magically washed away.

My freshman year ended, and onward came the much anticipated summer break. It's funny how summer break always seem so cool until after the first month has passed. The first month is full of various activities that can include family vacations, long weekend excursions, or just hanging out each day with friends. Though as the summer drags on, the activities seem to diminish, the days seem longer and just hanging out with friends gets a little boring. The summers were when I appreciated the church I went to. As I said before, we had a very large youth group each summer. This, of course, meant a summer full of various church activities. During those teenage years, I didn't act like a Christian unless I was at church. The pastor of the church had a daughter that was two years older than me. She was a beautiful girl. She and I snuggled next to each other on a bus ride returning to Texas from a church camp in Colorado. I was in love. Not the puppy dog type love I had heard about—no, this was true love. Unfortunately, her love for me ended as soon as we got off the bus. *Oh man, what happened?* I thought. *What must I do to get her back?* As if I ever had her in the first place.

A few weeks later, the church had an outdoor tent revival. The pastor's daughter, unlike me, did not sway in her Christian walk because of the company she was in. No, she was a good Christian who, on the first night of the revival, made a public rededication of her life to the Lord. I would have to say that my next decision was not led by the Holy Spirit. In fact, this was a significant turning point in my life. I remember thinking that since she made a public announcement of a personal decision, I should make one, too. Only, instead of just rededicating my life, I should do one better. I should get saved. After all, everyone would make a bigger deal out of me getting saved over a rededication. I now realize that using God's name in vain is more than just slipping up and saying "GD". Though I think that word is inappropriate and should never be used, I'm here to tell you that there are bigger ramifications behind using God's Word and His name for one's own personal gain. I believe this is what God meant when he gave the commandment to Moses. All I knew is that I wanted what I wanted, when I wanted it, and I was going to do whatever it took to get it.

So, on the second night of the revival, I got up in front of the congregation and announced how I had never truly accepted Christ as my savior. I went on and on about the wild debaucheries of a life of drug and alcohol abuse while on the high school golf team. I remember thinking how I was going to kill two birds with one stone. Not only would I win over the newfound love of my life, I would also relieve my parents with my life-changing decision. Well, things didn't go exactly as planned. Not only did I not get the girl, but I managed to make myself a target for ridicule from the most of the kids in school. Not to mention that most of the guys on the golf team wanted to kick my butt for bringing a lot of unwanted attention to them. Boy, I really made a mess of things with that decision. I remember thinking it wasn't a good idea to get up on stage and say all of that, because I knew I was doing it for all the wrong reasons, which would make it all a lie. Because of the overwhelming amount of ridicule I received, I completely went into the opposite direction. I convinced myself the best way to end the ridicule was to prove to everyone at my school that I wasn't some holy roller.

Nakot chuckled to himself as he nodded his head. "You stupid boy," he said. "I thought for a minute there I was going to lose you. Now, let's show them what a true party animal looks like."

Kansra appeared alongside Nakot and shared in the laughter at Carl's decision.

"So, we have another human who thinks if he just goes through the motions and recites a few words in the form of a prayer, he is truly saved."

"Yes, sire", replied Nakot. "His profession of faith was done for own self gain."

"I know," barked Kansra, "I can tell by his actions. I know he hasn't realized who Christ is and what it means to be born again, which means he is still ours to toy with. I've been watching your progress over the last several years. You were smart to influence him toward alcohol. The boy seems to feel inferior, so the alcohol will seem like a cure for that. That's definitely a good way to gain an edge with a challenging case. Now that the boy is responding well to the use of alcohol,

I want you to use the influence of his friends to introduce the harder drugs."

Nakot eagerly nodded his head. "Yes, sire, I enjoy watching these humans become our slaves in such a short amount of time. What used to take years with alcohol can be done in a few short months with the right drugs. I am being relentless in my pursuit of this soul. I will get him, sire."

"You better," replied Kansra as he left in a flash of light.

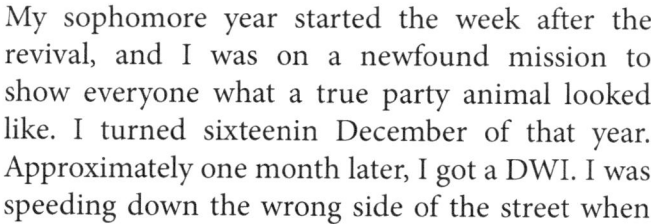

My sophomore year started the week after the revival, and I was on a newfound mission to show everyone what a true party animal looked like. I turned sixteen in December of that year. Approximately one month later, I got a DWI. I was speeding down the wrong side of the street when

I passed the cop. He later told me that he had to pull off the road to keep from colliding with me. I never saw him. He told my parents that I only got seven letters of the alphabet during my attempted recital. At the police station, I blew a .18 on the BAC machine. I was a very drunk sixteen-year-old kid, full of liquid courage, and was a total horse's butt to the police. I knew they were not going to physically hurt me, so I pushed the envelope. This was my first encounter with the cops; therefore, I didn't see the harm in acting like a fool. This was another bad idea.

The police didn't beat me up, but they sure remembered me. The town I was living in was pretty small, and they knew what kind of car I drove. I ended up with four MIPs (minor in possession of alcohol) by my senior year of high school. Life lesson learned: do not battle with the police. My DWI got me six months of juvenile probation. My new probation officer requested the presence of both my mother and my father for the viewing of my actions at the police station. After watching me act like a total smart-alecky punk kid, one that you would want to slap, my parents signed an agreement with the officer to basically rat me out in the event of a mess up. In other words, if I came drunk, there were supposed to call my probation officer so she could help them out with the discipline. My parents never had to rat me out, because each MIP got me another six months added to my probation sentence. I was not what you'd call a smooth criminal. My junior year came and went with not much excitement. I was getting drunk and high on weed, all while unsuccessfully trying to finish my probation.

Shortly after the beginning of my senior year, an old classmate of mine returned to the school. He had moved away at the beginning of our freshman year and had returned from abroad with some new and exciting experiences. "KD" is the name that I'll call my old buddy. KD and I would regularly smoke weed, and he would tell me of his adventures while living abroad with his father. KD was the kind of guy I thought I wanted to be. He never had any money, yet he was at every party riddled with party favors. He was good looking and smart, but carefree and dangerous. So there I was again, comparing myself to a friend and not measuring up, despite the truth that I was fairly popular among my peers. I was voted in the Senior Class Favorite and the Most Unpredictable. I was also nominated by the faculty of my high school to be awarded the very prestigious Outstanding High School Students of America Award. The school sent my information to Washington, along with a letter of recognition. I then received notice that I had been rewarded this award and that my name would go into the book of *Who's Who in America-1988*.

Through all this, I still felt inadequate and that I had something to prove. KD and I became close friends. He liked to smoke pot more than drink, so I developed a better liking for the high that accompanied marijuana. I'll never forget the night I found out my best friend was a junkie. I was riding in the back seat of a car being driven by a mutual friend of mine and KD's. I was very drunk that night and unable to drive my own car. We pulled into the parking lot of a restaurant alongside the small town's commonly known cruising strip. KD was standing beside a car in the parking lot, talking with several people. The girl driving the car I was in wanted to smoke a joint. KD always had weed. She called him over. I didn't participate in the joint, because I was very drunk and I was afraid it would make me sick. I had learned from past experience that if I smoked weed while I was drunk, I would start puking. After they finished the joint, the girl seemed stoned, but KD seemed to be something else.

Curiosity got the best of me, so I asked him, "Dude, what's up with you?"

He told me how great he felt because of how wired he was from shooting up something called *crystal*.

"What's crystal," I asked with obvious ignorance.

KD chuckled and said, "Crystal-meth—you know, methamphetamines." "Are you nuts?" I asked him.

"Yeah, probably," he jokingly replied. His nonchalant regard toward my reaction caught me off guard. I was shocked by what he had told me, but I was even more shocked at how open he was about it. "Bro, you should try it," he said with a grin.

"Man, you're crazy. I'm not shooting up," I replied. "Why not? What are you afraid of, man?"

"Dude, I'm scared of needles," I said.

"Bro, the needle is so small that you hardly feel it, and the high is better than anything you can imagine."

"I don't care, man; I'm not shooting up!"

Apparently the look in my eyes or the tone of my voice was convincing, because he rescinded his influential assault. He just laughed at me as he exited the vehicle, saying, "Bro, you don't know what you're missing."

I didn't shoot up that night, but a seed was planted. I was surprised, shocked, and angry that my friend was now a junkie. Though I was repulsed at the thought of shooting up, I was also very curious. I couldn't remove the image of how alert and alive he seemed to act. KD was the first person I knew to have actual experience with any drugs harder than weed. I had heard of cocaine and heroin before, but not methamphetamines. In the weeks to come, I asked KD a lot of questions about the effects of the various narcotics he had tried. He replied with nothing but praises about each and every one of them.

"Yes, yes, there you go boy, keep asking questions," said Nakot over and over. "You see how cool and popular KD is, and he's been doing the hard stuff for a while now. Stop acting like such a scared wimp. Come on now, don't you want to be the cool guy who courageously says, yes, while everyone else frightfully says, no!"

BAD TRIP

I TURNED EIGHTEEN ON THE 9THOF
December in 1987. In order for me to throw a
much-covered eightee-year-old birthday party,
I was going to have to hide it from my parents. I
decided to rent two joining rooms at a small, sleazy
motel. On December 18, I threw my party. I made
everyone enter into one room, where no alcohol was kept. If you wanted a beer from the keg,
which I had in the other room, you had to pay a
five-dollar cover fee. The party was a hit. In fact,
more people showed up than I expected. There was
a guy there that had graduated from my school a
few years prior. He had something called window-
pane acid. He gave me a hit of acid as a payment for
the cover fee. A guy I'll call "Buddy," who had been
a close friend for years, had just taken half a hit and
seemed very excited about it. He was drunk at the
time but told me he could feel the acid coming on
and that it felt awesome.

I know now that he was wrong about what he
was feeling. Acid takes longer than three minutes
to hit you. Also full of liquid courage, I decided

to take the whole hit. I put it under my tongue, as instructed. I remember thinking, *This is just a small piece of paper with no taste; maybe I got a bad one.* After about ten minutes, I went back to the guy and said that my hit didn't work. He laughed and said, "No problem, little dude. Here's another one for your troubles." I remember thinking that I had won on that deal, that he must have recognized who I was and had shown me the proper respect by freely giving me another hit. It turned out the joke was on me.

I had two hits of acid under my tongue and at least twelve large cups of beer in me when the cops decided to make their debut. My probation officer had told me that one more violation would land me in jail, that I would get no more probation extensions. The moment someone from the other room yelled "cops," I was flying out of the bathroom window. I ran across a field behind the motel and came out on a side street that led from the highway, which the motel sat beside, into a neighborhood. As I was exiting the field onto the side street, I saw my mother pulling off the highway into the parking lot of the motel. She had received a courtesy call from one of her friends stating that I had thrown a keg party at this motel and that the cops had been called.

I was never so happy to see my mother as I was at that moment. I immediately ran to her car, jumped into the front seat, and asked her to get me out of there. On the ride back to her house, the acid started to take effect, but I had forgotten that I took it. I was starting to trip at a very uncool time. My mother was beside herself, because there I was, drunk and high on something, throwing this party without a care in the world, knowing that if I got caught I would go to jail. She just kept saying, "What is wrong with you, son? Why are you doing this? Why are you trying to throw your life away?"

Because I was now starting to really trip on the acid, I started crying and saying, "I don't know, Mom. I don't know what's wrong with me, I'm sorry I'm not a good son." She drove me home, saying that I wasn't a bad son, but that I had some problems. As we pulled onto the long gravel driveway leading up to my mother's home, she told me that she was going to have to call my father about this.

I said, "No, you can't do that, because Dad said he was going to call my probation officer if I came in drunk again." Because this was the first time I had ever taken acid, I did not know what was happening to me. I was suddenly very strangely energetic, depressed, anxious, and fearless; yet I was terrified. My poor mother had to watch her son literally "trip out." I ran from the car inside the home, screaming that I was not going to jail. I ran into my bathroom, closed and locked the door, and started rummaging through the medicines in the closet. I took everything I could find.

My mother must have heard me, because she started knocking on the door, demanding to know what I was doing. I exited the bathroom, pushed passed my mother, and entered my bedroom. Her curiosity to know what I was doing in the bathroom drew her attention away from the fact that I had closed and locked my bedroom door behind me. By the time she realized that I was trying to commit suicide, I was slipping out of my bedroom window. She must have heard me falling out of the window, because she came running out the front door as I ran around the back of the house and into the woods. I'll never forget her crying and calling my name in the dark, pleading with me to come out of the woods.

Despite the blackness of the woods at night and my not having a light, I managed to slip around the house and back to the driveway. I had decided earlier to ride to my party with a friend. Because the cops all seemed to know my vehicle, I decided it best to leave my car at my mother's house so that it remained unseen that night. As I ran from the woods, I pulled the car keys from my pocket and prepared the ignition key, knowing that I must hurry because my mother would come running when she heard the car start.

I jumped into the driver seat, cranked it, put it in reverse, and floored it.

Apparently, she'd heard me running from the woods toward my car and realized what I was doing. I was unaware that she had run behind my car in an attempt to stop me from leaving. Thank God she realized I was oblivious to her whereabouts as I sped backward down the driveway. She had to jump out of the way to keep me from hitting her. When I saw her rolling in the grass off the front yard as I sped by, I stopped. As soon as I realized I had not hit her, I drove off into the night. My poor mother was left there in the grass, pleading and crying, not knowing if she would see her son alive again.

While I was driving through town, it seemed that headlights from the oncoming cars were excruciatingly bright. At a stoplight, I noticed the tires of the car next to me were melting and meshing with the lava-like pavement beneath us. Trees waved, spun, changed colors, and then resumed their form in cycles, as if in rhythm to some soundless music. Signs that normally sat beside the roads were not magically flowing in and out of traffic ahead of me. *I've got to get off the road*, I thought to myself. *I'll go to my work. No one will look for me there, and there's a bottle of Valium in the boss's office that will definitely put me out of my misery.*

I wasn't sure of what all I had taken at my mother's house, but I wanted to take more of something to ensure that I succeeded at this suicide attempt. I had started working at an animal hospital about one year prior to this night. Part of my daily duties at the clinic was to put the animals out on the runs while I cleaned their cages. I was a kennel boy. I would do this every afternoon and on weekends when the clinic was closed, hence the reason behind my possessing a key. In addition to taking care of the animals, I also would empty the trash, sweep, and mop the entire clinic. I was a couple of weeks prior to this night that, while snooping through the doctor's desk, I had come across a bottle of ten milligram Valium. I wasn't sure of the effect or of how many to take of the drug in order to get high; therefore, I put the bottle back where I found it in hopes I could find someone who knew something about it. I had completely forgotten about the find until now. Like I said, I wasn't sure of the effects of Valium, but I was pretty sure that I had heard its name in association with pill overdoses.

The clinic sat right alongside the main highway running through the town. Obviously, I wouldn't be working at midnight on a Friday night' therefore, I had to park my car in a neighborhood nearby and sneak in through the dark. This was especially challenging in the state of mind I was in. Crawling through the tall grass of the ditch line, which paralleled the highway, was an idea that should have stayed just that—an idea. Terrifying hallucinations usually accompany a bad trip, which I can say that I was definitely having; therefore, things that were not there suddenly came to life. The grass became a bed of snakes I was immersed into. So much for the need to remain stealthy while sneaking into the clinic. The thought of crawling through snakes was more than I could handle. Out of the grass I came, screaming and hollering and running for the clinic door. As I crossed the parking lot, I pulled the front door key from my pocket, thinking that I could open the door and get inside before anyone drove by and saw me.

"Hahaa," I proudly cried as I locked the door behind me. "Nobody saw me, right," I said to myself as I peered through the glass door and into the parking lot. At least five minutes passed while I laid there in the dark, gazing out at the cars passing by on the highway, hoping and praying not to see that bright red glow that accompanies the hard braking of a vehicle. Once I was satisfied that I was alone and going to stay that way, I left the front lobby and headed back to the doctor's office. Much to my alarmed surprise, the bottle of much-needed Valium was gone from the desk drawer. I frantically searched throughout the entire office, thinking maybe the doc had just moved them around for whatever reason. *I can't believe this,* I thought. *Now what am I going to do?*

A sense of panic started coming over me. I was afraid I had taken only enough pills at my mother's to make me very sick, but probably not enough to kill me. I don't know why I wanted to end it all that night. It was as if some dark force was driving me, telling me, "This will show everyone, and they'll be sorry."

Instead of going to the clinic's pharmacy, where there were more than enough drugs to do me in, I decided to raid the employee bathroom's medicine cabinet. I quickly stepped from the doctor's office into the bathroom. I turned on the light and froze. The mirror of the medicine cabinet reflected a haunting image. The face resembled my face, yet it was terrifyingly different. My face appeared longer than normal, as if my chin extended down four to five inches below my bottom lip. My cheekbones were raised, and my cheeks seemed to be drawn in on both sides, as if I had eaten a bowl of persimmons. Of all the scary yet interesting features of my new face, it was my eyes that drew my attention the most. I took the last to steps that separated me from the bathroom sink in an attempt to see what was behind my eyes. It appeared that in place of my eyes were two perfectly round, black holes that would lead into my brain.

The longer I stared at my reflection, the more lost in my face I became.

Suddenly, I snapped back to reality, the reality that I was on a mission and that I was in the bathroom for a reason. I threw open the medicine cabinet, hoping to make a grand discovery like the one I made in the doctor's office. "Maybe he moved the bottle of Valium from his desk to the bathroom," I said to myself.

Much to my disappointment though, instead of a bottle of Valium I found a bottle of aspirin. There was an unopened 300-count bottle of Bayer Aspirin on the top shelf. "Ohh well!" is all I said as I opened the bottle and started consuming the contents. I used water from the sink to wash down the aspirin. I don't remember how many handfuls it took, only that except for the few that fell on the floor, I swallowed the entire bottle. I dropped the bottle in the trash, took one last look at myself in the mirror, and decided to bolt. I was afraid I might be discovered at the clinic; therefore, I needed to make a run for it.

In the dark, I crawled through the lobby to peer out the front door. Once I was satisfied that the coast was clear, I ran from the clinic back into the neighborhood to my car. "Maybe the coast is clear at the room I rented," I said to myself as I started my journey across town. The task of driving while tripping had not gotten any easier, except this time, the reality of what I was doing kept my focus off the dancing lights and trees. As I pulled off the highway into the neighborhood behind the motel, I scanned the parking lot to make sure there was no one there looking for me. The lot was dark and empty; there were no signs of any unwanted visitors lurking about, waiting to pounce on me if I came out of the shadows. In all, I made three passes around the motel before parking my car on a side street back off in the neighborhood.

In one quick motion, I leapt from the car, ran up the street and through the field, and crawled back through the bathroom window I had escaped from earlier. The keg was still in the second room. The cops didn't find it. Everyone that came to the party had to enter into the first room and then knock on the door of the adjoining room in order to get a beer from the keg. When the cops raided the place, they didn't know to check the second room. The reason I know all of this is because, as

I came crawling through the bathroom window, I was greeted by my friend Buddy. He filled me in on the details as we sat down at the table to enjoy a much-needed beer.

Buddy had only taken a half a hit of acid; therefore, his tripping experience was much more manageable for him than mine was for me. As I was sitting there intently listening to him boasting about his near miss with the cops, I suddenly began to feel very strange. An unknown and somewhat frightening feeling started rushing over me. My vision blurred, and then Buddy's voice started to fade, drowned out by a popping and crackling noise. As if this wasn't bad enough, here came the instant, overwhelming sense of nausea that meant my body was trying to get rid of what I had put into it. The first time I threw up was excruciatingly relieving. The vomit was comprised of large amounts of undigested aspirin and beer and water. When the feeling of nausea hit me, I ran into the bathroom and closed the door before I started to barf so Buddy could not see the contents of my puke. Not that he would have wanted to anyway. After a couple of minutes of serious barfing, I emerged from the bathroom laughing and saying, "Yeah, now it's a party."

Buddy joined in with the laughter. "Dude, I thought I was going to have to find someone to go in there and help you dig your stomach back out of the toilet." We both laughed as I poured another beer and rejoined him at the table. About thirty minutes passed before the feeling hit me again. I repeated the earlier performance and thought surely that would be it. Boy, was I wrong. I threw up thirteen times over the next six hours before Buddy convinced me to call my parents for help. *Maybe he's right,* I thought to myself. *This whole suicide thing is too long and painful.*

My mother answered her phone on the first ring with an alarmed, "Hello?" Bless her heart; she had spent the entire night searching the town trying to find me. While she prayed that this phone call was from me, she had a very real fear that it was the police, saying they had found her son dead. Within minutes, both my mother and father arrived at the motel room. Before I could even tell them how sick I was, my mother drew both her hands up to cover her face and started to cry.

I was pale white, very dizzy, and dangerously dehydrated. Standing up and remaining upright was more than I could handle. My mother realized that her son was in trouble, regained her composure, and helped me get into her car. Before I could close the car door, I had to puke again. I leaned out of the car and started trying to throw up. The problem was that there was nothing left in my stomach wall, because instead of beer, I was now throwing up clots of bloody bile. After what seemed like twenty minutes of straining to remove the poisons from my stomach, I was able to finally stop lurching. There was a dinner-plate-sized pool of blood beside the car. Seeing this caused my mother to start crying again, but I was too weak to try to comfort her. I wanted to comfort her, to tell her that everything was going to be all right. I wanted to tell her how sorry I was for almost running over her the night before. In fact, I wanted the night before to rewind. What was I thinking? I didn't want to die.

"What did you take, Carl? Son, what all did you take?" were the questions my mother kept asking me as she rapidly drove me to the hospital. I just laid there in the front seat of her car, staring out the passenger window at the houses rushing by, thinking, *God, what have I done?*

My father, who was in his car in front of us, arrived at the hospital shortly before we did. By the time we pulled up, there was a nurse with a wheelchair waiting on the sidewalk beside my father. We pulled to a stop in front of the nurse, but before she could reach out toward the door, I flung it open and started puking up more blood and bile. Alarmed by the site of this, she called for help. As soon as I stopped lurching, I was quickly transferred from the car to the wheelchair and escorted into the emergency room. They wheeled me into a private room, where the doctor asked my parents what was wrong with me. My mother pulled out a Ziploc bag filled with empty packets of medicine samples as well as a couple of emptied prescription bottles. She told the doctor I had taken all of the mediations that were in those packets and bottles and that I had probably taken something else, but she didn't know what. "Aspirin," I finally said, "I took three hundred aspirin."

The room fell silent while everyone stared at me with a look like, "Why would you do that? Are you crazy?"

"Aspirin? Why would you take three hundred aspirin?" asked my father. "What were you trying to do, kill yourself?"

The doctor chimed into the conversation at that point and said to my parents, "Can I speak to y'all outside for a moment?" The doctor gave the nurse and order to start me on an IV of fluids and give me something called Phenergan to calm the nausea. Outside the room, the doctor asked my parents specifics about the night before. He needed to know what all I had taken and how long ago I had taken it.

My father stuck his head through the door and asked, "Son, what all did you take, and how long ago did you take the aspirin?"

"I took two hits of acid, whatever was in mom's medicine closet, and the aspirin all around midnight last night." The doctor heard my answer and said that too much time had passed for them to pump my stomach. He then walked over to my bed.

"Carl, are you having thoughts of suicide? Do you want to cause harm to yourself?"

"No," I responded. "I don't know why I took all that stuff. I can't remember much after the acid." I could tell by the way the doctor was asking me these questions that my response had better be to denounce any coherent thoughts of suicide, so I did. He told my parents he was going to write this up as an accidental overdose instead of a suicide attempt. In his opinion, I simply had a back reaction to the LSD, that I probably would not have taken all that stuff if I wasn't on a bad trip. I would have had to go to a psych ward for evaluation if we had written it up as a suicide attempt, and no one wanted that.

After studying the empty containers of the meds I had taken at my mother's, he told my parents that by taking one of the meds, I had actually helped preserve my stomach walls. I believe a guardian angel was watching out for me, because I had taken eighteen prescription-strength antacids in my futile attempts to overload my system. The antacids helped coat my stomach walls and suppress the volatile reaction the aspirin would have had with my stomach acids, therefore, the damage was minimal. The doctor told us I was going to be all right but that he would like for me to stay the night at the hospital so they could continue administering the fluids and make sure no unexpected problems arose. It was as if, while telling my parents he had given me something to help me rest, the Phenergan the nurse had just given me suddenly overwhelmed me, and I comfortably drifted off to sleep.

Nakot shook his head as he paced back and forth in the corner of the hospital room. "Ahh," he screamed, "I was so close!"

Kansra appeared next to Nakot with a heavy scowl on his face. "Why is that boy still alive? Why didn't you convince him to enter the pharmacy?"

"I tried, sire," Nakot quickly replied. "He did not respond to the numerous attempts I made. I don't understand why I lost control all of a sudden. He was in the clinic, I had him convinced the only way out of this mess was death, that it would make his parents sorry for not indulging him, and was pushing him toward the pharmacy when he just— just left. I mean, it was as if one minute I had him, and the next minute, none of my influence seemed to work."

Kansra looked over at Carl asleep in the bed and paused for a moment before he asked, "Was there an angel there?"

"None that I could see, sire," Nakot replied as he turned his head and looked at the floor. After a small pause of silence, Nakot turned back toward Kansra. "Although, that would explain my loss of control. But this boy hasn't truly confessed his sins and asked Christ to be his Savior; therefore, he is not a child of God. So why would God send and angel to protect him?"

Now Kansra turned away for a moment before replying in an unsure voice, "I don't know. Maybe it's the boy's parents and grandparents that are praying for him. Or maybe there was no angel. You said you didn't actually see one—right?"

"That's right, sire," Nakot said. "It's possible that my influence was overwhelmed by the effects of the drugs he was on."

Kansra chuckled. "Yeah, that's right. The stupid boy was on LSD. It's one of my favorites. It doesn't usually kill them as quickly as cocaine or heroin, but I enjoy seeing them slowly lose their minds. It's an anything-goes kind of scenario when they're on LSD. I guess that could explain your loss on control."

A grin full of relief flashed across Nakot's grotesque face. "Thank you, sire. I was afraid you'd be angry with me. I didn't get him this time, but don't worry; it's just a matter of time."

"No, you fool!" Kansra whirled on the now-cowering demon. "Time is not a luxury you can afford. That boy has parents and grandparents that are part of Christ's church. They are born-again believers who are constantly praying for the boy. If you don't hurry up and get him, their influence might start him searching for the truth. Now, I want you to turn up the heat. You need to treat every day as if you might not have another. Do you understand what I'm telling you?"

Nakot quickly nodded his head. "Yes, sire. He seems to be responding well to the influence of drugs. Hopefully soon, he will overdose or succeed with a suicide attempt."

"For your sake, I hope so, Nakot," Kansra growled as he turned to leave. He paused before turning back to Nakot. "A word of advice, Nakot. These actions the boy has taken are going to bring a lot of unwanted attention from his family. He will, no doubt, feel some remorse for these events. It will be up to you to convince him that it's not the drugs that are the problem. Tell him he was the victim of a freak experience, a one-time bad trip. You're going to have to improve your skills. LSD or no LSD, there's no excuse for you losing the boy when you had him on the ropes like that."

Before Nakot could reply, Kansra was gone. The shame Nakot felt was quickly replaced by a boiling anger. "Boy, you're making me look bad. When you do finally kill yourself, I'm going to request that I'm able to escort your soul to hell and remain there as your personal tormentor for the next century. Oh, I can't wait to get you."

THE GRIP OF METHAMPHETAMINES

I WAS GROUNDED FROM THE CAR THAT my father had bought me for a while. He didn't give me a definite time frame, and given the circumstances, I didn't ask. He told me that because I was now eighteen years old, I was too old to be grounded, but since he had bought the car and it was in his name, I couldn't use it to get around. I was just happy to be allowed out of the house. I remember thinking; *This whole not-being-grounded thing is going to be pretty cool.*

None of my friends knew anything about my suicide attempt or even that I had ended up at the hospital. I was embarrassed and was glad no one knew. My parents, bless their hearts, wanted to believe this was a one-time, freak experience. KD lived about a mile away from Dad's house, which was perfect, since my only modes of transportation were walking and my skateboard. I started walking or riding my board over to his house almost every afternoon to smoke pot and hang out. His mother worked late most days, so we had the house to ourselves. We would smoke weed, and KD would harass me about shooting up.

He would laugh at me and how adamant I was. He would laughingly say, "Dude, I'm going to shoot you up with some speed, and you're going to love it."

Assuredly I would reply, "No way, man, I'll never do that!"

"Yes, you will!" "No, I won't!"

Back and forth we'd go, but I knew it was harmless, because he didn't have any speed. He just liked getting a rise out of me. Two weeks went by from my infamous birthday party weekend to the weekend that changed everything for me. It was a Friday night, and I still had no car to drive. I called KD; he invited me over to his house. He told me he was with a buddy of his and that I needed to hurry up and get over there, that he had something cool to show me. I hung up the phone and told my dad I was going over to KD's house but that I would be home by 1:00 a.m. This was the curfew my father asked me to honor. He said if I was going to stay out past that time, then I needed to stay there all night, but I needed to let him know before he went to bed. I quickly walked to KD's house wondering what he was talking about—*What cool thing does he have to show me?*

As I walked up the street and into the front yard of KD'S home, I noticed his mother's car was gone, but a familiar old truck was parked in the driveway. I knocked on the door and heard a lot of commotion coming from inside. After a moment, my attention was caught by the blinds of the window next do the door. KD peered out through the opening before I heard him announce to someone that it was just me. He finally opened the door and looked past me at the road as he told me to hurry and come inside.

"What's up, bro? Where you been?" he asked.

Before I could reply by saying, Man, I just talked to you like twenty minutes ago," my attention was caught by someone walking into the living room from one of the bedrooms. It was a guy a couple of years older than us who had dropped out of high school and had the reputation of being a pretty rough guy. I remember being a little intimidated by his presence, but of course, I would never let either one of them know of my nervousness.

They seemed to be occupied with something; they were wiring up speakers throughout the house and talking so fast that I quit trying to keep up. "Hey, dudes, y'all want to smoke a joint?" I asked as I pulled a sack of weed from my jacket pocket.

"Yeah, sure, man," was replied, yet neither one of them looked in my direction.

"Cool, I'll roll a fatty." I rolled a ridiculously fat joint in hopes to gain their recognition and approval. I lit it and walked into the kitchen, where they were sitting at the table, dissecting a portable boom box stereo. "What are y'all doing?" I asked as I tried to pass KD the joint.

Big A was the nickname KD's new friend was going by. He had no sat stillor said very much since I'd walked in. he intercepted the joint, took a couple of really big hits, handed the joint back to me, and leaned his head over to see what KD was doing.

Without looking up, KD said, "I'm trying to splice this speaker wire directly into the wires that supply the stereos speakers so I can hook up my large speakers to this small stereo and have some ridiculously loud sound."

As I turned to walk away, I said, "Yeah, okay, man, whatever. Well, are you going to smoke this joint with me or what?"

Without changing his focus, KD said, "Yeah, man, we'll be there in a minute."

I left the kitchen and returned to the living room, where I sat down and started smoking the joint by myself. This was some really strong weed, and because I wasn't what you'd call a real pot head, I started getting really stoned. "Ohh, yeah, say man, what's this cool stuff you said you had to show me?" I asked as I stood from the couch and staggered back to the kitchen.

KD and Big A started whispering for a moment. Then as Big A gave a nodding approval, KD looked at me, grinned, and said, "Man, I've got something for you." Suddenly, the seriousness of dissecting his boom box seemed less interesting to him. I watched him rise from the table, walk to his refrigerator, and pull out of the freezer several small, odd-shaped plastic bags filled with something yellow. As he walked closer, I could see that he had cut the corners off of clear sandwich bags and filled each one with a small amount of what looked like a tiny piece of a wet, yellow soap bar.

"What is that?" I asked as he held up a single package and shook it in front of my face.

"This is the stuff I've been telling you about. You ready to try it?" KD said with a half-cocked smile.

"This is the stuff that you've been shooting up?" I asked as I looked from him to Big A. I was a little embarrassed that it was so obvious that this was the first time I had ever seen methamphetamines.

He laughed, looked at Big A, then back at me. "Yeah, man this is the good stuff. So what's up? Do you want a shot?" Fear gripped me, a fear of the reality of what was happening and what he was asking me to do.

"No, man, I'm cool with my weed and beer," I reluctantly said as I left them in the kitchen and returned to the living room. They just laughed as they sat back down at the table and returned to reconstructing the radio. In the living room, I sat down on the couch, picked up the half-smoked joint, and re-lit it. I was embarrassed that I was so afraid of what they seemed so nonchalant about. As I sat there finishing the joint, a persuasive voice entered my head. *Dude, it's probably not that big of a deal. You know, I bet the only reason people tell you not to shoot up is because of how good it will make you feel. I mean, look at* them; they're all right. In fact, they look like they're having fun.

As these thoughts were racing through my mind, I started to realize I was way more stoned than I wanted to be. I looked into the kitchen and saw KD and Big A full of excitement and energy, seemingly ready to take on the world, and here I was, about to fall off the couch. "How much does it take to get high?" I asked.

"A quarter-gram shot is what I did," KD replied. There was an uncomfortable moment of silence as I sat there battling with myself to stop asking these leading questions.

"How much is a quarter gram?" I finally asked.

Again, KD answered from the kitchen. "Each one of these baggies is a quarter, and they cost twenty-five dollars each."

And again, I felt that uncomfortable silence as I sat there realizing I had run out of leading questions, that it was time to make a decision. Was I going to do this or what?

Come on, Carl, just do one shot, and you'll feel as good as they do, was a voice resounding in my mind. It's amazing how similar that sounds to "Come on, Eve, just take one bite, and you'll know all that God knows."

After a minute or so, this persuasive voice got the best of me, and I stepped onto a road that has taken me twenty-two years to crawl back off of.

"Hey, man, I've got twenty-five dollars. Will you hook me up?" I asked as I got up from the couch and walked back into the kitchen. KD looked at Big A and chuckled as he rose from the table to start gathering the items he needed to perform the task I was asking of him. He grabbed a large spoon from a drawer beside the sink and filled a glass with water. He placed them on the table and instructed me to sit down in his chair while he went to get a Q-tip from the bathroom.

Big A pulled one of the packages from the freezer, untied the twist tie, and poured the contents into a spoon lying on the table in front of me. KD returned from the bathroom with the Q-tip and a thin syringe with a bright orange cap. I had never known any diabetics; therefore, I had never seen a syringe that small. The only syringes I had ever seen were the larger ones used by doctors. I remember feeling a sense of relief when I saw this thin syringe and its tiny needle. I thought, *Maybe KD was telling the truth when he said it doesn't hurt.*

Like a good student, I paid close attention to every detail KD was doing to break down and draw up the dope. The second he expelled the last air bubble, he looked at me and said, "Let's go." It felt as if butterflies were doing back flips inside my stomach as I started rolling up the sleeve of my left arm. KD instructed me to grip my left bicep with my right hand and start to squeeze. At the same time, I started pumping my left fist, causing the veins in my left arm to rise up and make for an easy target. Though part of me didn't want to watch, I couldn't take my eyes off the needle as he lined it up directly over a large vein in the crease of my arm. I couldn't help but tense up a little as he started pushing the needle through the skin and into my vein. There was only a mild bite and little burn as the needle disappeared into my arm. He started pulling back the plunger, which started drawing my blood into the barrel. Without looking up, he told me, "You've always got to register to make sure you're in the vein. If you're not in the vein, then you won't get any blood when you pull back on the plunger."

"Well, what happens if I don't shoot it into the vein?" I asked him.

"Dude, you don't want to do that. Trust me, it will set your arm on fire," he replied before asking if I was ready. Before I answered, he started pushing the solution into my vein. At the very moment the plunger zeroed, he pulled the needle from my arm. I was overwhelmed by a sudden, strange chemical taste and an uncontrollable urge to cough. As I leaned forward and coughed, a strong wave of sensations overcame me. It was as if the hairs on the back of my neck and head stood up and caught on fire. My vision blurred, things in front of me started shaking from side to side, and everything got quiet for a moment. I couldn't seem to catch my breath, but I suddenly felt the need to stand and move around.

KD started laughing as he asked, "Dude, are you all right?"

I left the kitchen and started pacing the floor of the living room, trying to get a grasp on the flood of all the new and awesome pleasurable sensations.

"Dude, are you all right?"

"Ohh, yeah!" I replied. "Man, this is awesome," was all I could say as I packed the floors until the rush subsided a bit. I was full of energy and excitement and ready to do a hundred things all at the same time. *Man, everything they said about this stuff is a lie; something this good can't be wrong,* were the words that resounded in my mind. Nothing in all my imagining came even close to this newfound friend called methamphetamines.

KD and Big A pointed and laughed at me circling the living room as if they were the proud parents of an infant learning to walk. I looked around the room but couldn't find anything I wanted to get into, so I suggested we go ride around town in search of some action.

Big A whispered something to KD, and then KD addressed me. "All right, dude, we'll go to town; but you've got to slow down a little bit."

"What are you talking about, man? I'm cool."

"No, you're not; it's obvious you're on it. You've got to stop looking so excited and talking and moving so fast. You don't want everyone knowing you're doing this stuff because someone will end up telling the cops; then they'll start watching you even more than they do now."

His words sunk in, and I assured him that no one would know. We loaded up into Big A's truck and headed for town. It was as if this was the first time I had been allowed to go to town for months. I felt so excited, but I was cautious not to let it show. The night air was clear and cold and I felt great. Even the music Big A was playing seemed to have meaning to me—I could feel the music. There was nothing exciting happening in town that night, so I returned home at 1:00a.m. like I told my dad I would. I couldn't sleep, so I spent the night in my room reorganizing everything.

The next day came, and though I swore to KD that I would tell no one, I seemingly couldn't help but call my friends Buddy and JJ. I mean, I had to share this newfound experience with them. What kind of friend would I be if I didn't let them in on this secret? My father surprised me that day with the news that I could start using my car again as long as I turned the keys in to him each night and didn't exceed the curfew. This was especially great news and good timing because Buddy did not have a car and JJ had a small Ford Ranger pickup with just a single cab.

It was about 1:00 p.m. when I called them and told them I had regained possession of my car and asked them if they wanted to go out that night. They each said yes, so I agreed to pick them up around 7:00 p.m. As soon as I got off the phone, I decided to go to KD's to make arrangements to get some more of that "good stuff."

KD was home alone, piddling around the house, still amped up from the night before. I told him of my plans to get high with Buddy and JJ and that I was going to need three of those quarter packages. At first, he was skeptical about my assuredness that Buddy and JJ were going to be cool with it, but after a small amount of coercion, he caved and made a phone call. I think he decided he wanted to get some, too, and that he only needed ten dollars to add to my seventy-five dollars in order to get a gram (four quarters).

Later that day, KD and I took a drive into the country, about ten miles from town. We pulled off the highway onto a long dirt driveway riddled with potholes that seemed to wind its way back off into the deep woods. After several minutes,

I began to wonder if we were traveling on an oversized four-wheeler trail, which would eventually arrive at a hunting camp. Then suddenly, the trees opened up to reveal an old, rundown trailer house sitting atop a small hill, surrounded by an array of junk.

When I say "junk", I mean junk. There were probably fourteen or fifteen old broken-down washers and dryers, half a dozen different types of refrigerators, several remnants of old cars and trucks, and the list go on and on. A sense of apprehension rushed through me as I looked at the trailer and its surroundings and felt as if I had been transposed into the movie *Deliverance*. "What-tha?" is all I could say as I kind of chuckled in order to hide the nervousness I was feeling.

Apparently KD had experienced similar feelings on his first encounter with this place, because he quickly assured me there was nothing to fear and that he would be inside only for a moment. I gave him my seventy-five dollars, and as instructed, I remained in the car, left alone with my thoughts and these strange, somewhat haunting surroundings. This place was truly like something from a bad dream. Each window of the trailer was completely covered by aluminum foil except for a few strategically placed peepholes so that someone could peer out.

I dared not stare at any one place on the trailer for too long, for fear that a very large, very hairy guy might come running out accusing me of trying to figure out what was going on inside. Relief swept over me the moment KD came walking out the front door. I casually looked but saw n o one inside as the door quickly closed and locked behind him. Though I was curious to see what type of person lived in this environment, I was somewhat relieved that no eye contact was made. "Let's go," KD said before he could even close the door of the car.

"Did you get it?" I asked as I put the car in reverse.

"Yeah, I got it. Check this out," he said as he pulled out a baggie with a large beige rock inside.

Excitement pulsed through my veins. "Buddy and JJ are going to love this stuff," I said to myself as I reminisced about how awesome the shot I had done made me feel. KD told me he had a date that night with a girl I knew; therefore, he would not be partying with me and the guys. We went back to his house to break up the gram. I watched as he poured the contents of the baggie onto a plate and set it on the table. He took out his driver's license and started crushing the rock, which caused it to turn into powder. After chopping his way through the pile of powder several times with his license, he raked it into the form of a rectangle. Then he separated the rectangle into four separate but even-sized piles and said, "There you go. You get which-ever three you want."

"Cool, man, I appreciate it," I said and then remembered, "Ohh, yeah, dude, I need some of those needles."

He laughed. "Points, man, they're called points, not needles." He then instructed me on how to buy syringes and which pharmacy would sell them to me without any questions.

I left his house and went home to change my clothes. I was wearing some jeans with the knees torn from them and a long black duster over a jean jacket over a plain white tee shirt. I had raggedy black boots on my feet and weight lifters' gloves on my hands. I had seen the movie *The Breakfast Club* too many times and thought I wanted to look like Jud Nelson, but this was not appropriate attire for purchasing "points" without drawing some unwanted attention. Nice jeans and a polo shirt ought to do it, I thought as I rummaged through my closet and prepared myself for the task ahead of me. I rehearsed the lines KD had given me on the way to the pharmacy, making sure I could say them without stuttering or stammering or in any way say them without confidence. Butterflies started dancing in my stomach the moment I pulled into the parking lot of the pharmacy.

"Okay, man, you can do this," I told myself. As I walked to the counter, I was somewhat relieved that it was just a young sales girl and not an overbearing, intimidating pharmacist.

"Can I help you?" she said.

All right, man, here we go, I thought as I said, "Yes, ma'am." I then told her what I wanted and, surprisingly, she gave me no funny looks as she turned and walked away. Moments later, she returned carrying a small, clear package filled with ten syringes. I paid the clerk, turned, and triumphantly walked out of the pharmacy. "Wow, that was a lot easier than I thought," I said to myself as I pulled out of the parking lot and headed home to get ready for the night.

Buddy and JJ had never shot up before, but given their curiosity toward drugs, I figured they would try it once they saw me do it. I picked each of them up around 7:00 that night and headed for town. On the ride, I told them I was still high from meth I had done the night before, and it was the best feeling I had ever experienced.

"No way, man. You didn't save us any?" Buddy asked.

Before I could answer, JJ asked, "How did you do it?" I had told them about the times KD had tried to get me to shoot meth with him, and though I had rehearsed my intended lines of coercion, I felt my stomach drop when posed with that question.

"I shot it," is all I could say. "Did it hurt?" asked Buddy.

"No, man, it didn't hurt at all, and the rush you get is indescribable." There was an uncomfortable pause of silence, which led me to believe they were pondering the idea. "Do y'all want to try it?" I asked. There was another uncomfortable pause of silence, which was finally broken by their whispering between each other.

A smile came across my face when JJ asked, "Why, do you have some?" "Yeah, I've got three quarters and ten points," I proudly replied.

Buddy looked at JJ briefly before asking, "What are quarters, and what are points?"

I started answering their questions as if I had known these things for years. "Quarters are a quarter of a gram, and points are what we call syringes. A quarter is all it takes to get high. I bought three quarters today for the three of us. Now, I'm going to shoot one of them. You can see what it does for me; then you decide if you want to try it or not."

They agreed to try it, so I suggested that we head to the animal hospital to perform the act. I parked the car in the same neighborhood, and the three of us headed down the street. Again, I paused for a break in traffic before we dashed across the parking lot and slipped inside the door. Once I was sure we had entered without being seen, we headed back to one of the exam rooms to start the process. I grabbed a large spoon from the employee break area and filled a coffee mug with warm water before sitting at a stool I had placed beside the stainless steel exam table. I removed the three individually wrapped quarters from a box of cigarettes I pulled from my jacket pocket. I started imitating the actions I had seen KD perform the night before. I wasn't sure if I could hit myself, so I started giving instructions to Buddy on the proper technique of shooting me up.

He looked at me and emphatically said, "No way, man, I'm not shooting you up."

I'd started to reassure him that it would be okay and that I would guide him through the process, when JJ said, "It's cool, man, I'll do it." I was relieved that he agreed to help me; otherwise, I wasn't sure how we'd proceed. With the help of my instruction, he was able to complete the task, and once again, I was off to the races. Upon seeing how wired I was and that nothing bad resulted from it, they each became very eager to try it. I took joy in watching their reactions to the drug and realized how KD and Big A must have felt when they witnessed mine.

I shot up JJ first and then Buddy and laughed as they ran around the clinic full of excitement, energy and a newfound resolution to make sure we got more of the stuff. We left the clinic and decided to cruise around town looking for some action. Keep in mind, this was a small town, and as usual, there was no action to be found. After riding around for about three hours, JJ suggested we go to his house, take his mother's keys, and go run around inside the high school.

JJ's mother worked in the office of the high school as the treasurer, and therefore had a master set of keys which could open every door. Apparently he and Buddy had done this before, because Buddy chimed in excitedly at that point, saying, "Yeah, man, that's a good idea. Don't worry, dude, there's no alarm or anything."

Their confidence in this idea assured me that they must know what they were talking about. And besides, it did sound like a lot of fun, so to JJ's house we went. Buddy and I remained in the car, parked down the street, while J quietly slipped inside to take his mother's keys. After a couple of minutes, he came walking up the street with a victorious grin on his face. He jumped in the car, and we headed for the school. As instructed, I parked the car on a street that ran parallel with the school but was separated by an overgrown field. We slipped through the tall grass toward the back of the building. JJ said he could open any door with the key he was holding, but we should go to the back of the school because it was much less visible.

We ran from the tall grass cover, across the football practice field, and through the back door in one quick, fluid-like motion. We immediately

ran from the back of the school to the front windows. The entire front-entrance area of the school
was made of glass; therefore, we could see both
entrance drives to the school and make sure no one
had pulled onto the campus in pursuit of us. After
a moment, we realized the coast was clear and we
could freely wander about the school. Though I
had gone to this school for three and a half years
and had been inside almost every room, the school
suddenly felt new and exciting, as if behind every
door was a possible adventure. Eventually, the
excitement started wearing off and the rooms of
new possibilities turned back into the same old
classrooms we attended everyday.

"Let's go to the office," JJ suggested.

"Ohh, yeah," Buddy and I said at the same
time. The office was the one place I had never freely
roamed, meaning there were endless possibilities of
new things to whet my curious appetite. The security lights were on in the office, which provided
enough light for us to see our way around. After
being inside the office for only a moment, I noticed
a very large vault door. It was standing at the end
of a short hallway, centered between the principal's
office and the treasurer's—or JJ's mom's—office. It
stood about seven feet high and four feet wide and
appeared to be very thick and heavy. The door was
wrought iron, black with brass trim and a brass turn
wheel, which when turned to the left, would retract
the large latching pin from its surrounding frame.

"Hey, JJ, what's in there?" I asked as I examined the door and its surroundings.

"It's the school vault; what do you think is in there? Money!" JJ sarcastically replied.

Embarrassed, I said, "Well, I know there's money in there. I mean how much money, do you think, is in there?"

"Probably not that much, since it's the weekend. My mom usually makes a deposit at the bank on Friday."

"Well, let's see if we can get in there anyway," I said as I observed the combination keypad located just to the right of the turn wheel. JJ must have known what I was thinking, because he told me I couldn't start randomly punching in numbers. If I made three wrong entries, the system would lock out and they would know someone was trying to break into it.

"Hmm, well, let's start looking for the combination," I said as I turned and walked into the principal's office. Buddy, JJ, and I relentlessly searched each office but found nothing that resembled a combination code. While they were searching through JJ's mother's office, I, on a hunch, decided to climb onto her desk, lift a ceiling tile, and see what was up there. I strained to see but could not. I was going to need a flashlight in order to explore past the ceiling grid.

JJ noticed what I was trying to do and left his mother's office, attempting to locate a flashlight. I got down from the desk and accompanied Buddy in joining in the search. We pilfered through every office and storage closet but were unsuccessful in finding a flashlight. JJ was suggesting we go to the chemistry lab to search when Buddy came out of an office with a small lamp and a six-foot extension cord.

"Perfect, bro, good job," I said as I headed for the treasurer's office. I climbed back onto the desk while they plugged in the lamp and removed the shade. The desk I was standing on was resting against a painted cinderblock wall, which I knew to be an exterior wall of the vault. I asked for a chair to stack on the desk so I could stand up through the ceiling grid and, using the light, see if I could find a way into the vault through the top. Sure enough, there it was, located about three feet above the grid: a hole in the cinderblock wall.

Apparently, when they ran the electrical and sprinkler piping into the vault, they forgot to replace the several blocks that were removed. It wasn't a very large hole, but I knew I could squeeze through when the time was right—which which was not right then. None of us were sure the vault door could be opened from the inside; therefore, I would need some way to climb back out. Besides that, even if we got into the vault, we couldn't take anything, because we used keys to get inside the school. The three of us decided that we were going to get into that vault, but we needed to plan it for another night. I guess I had seen enough crime movies, because I suggested we wipe down everything we touched so that we left no prints behind. Once satisfied we were leaving the school without a trace, we exited the back door, ran across the fields, and returned safely to my car. We resumed cruising around the town while we discussed the possibilities of what we could do with a thousand or so dollars. My curfew was still 1:00 a.m., so I drove Buddy and JJ back to Buddy's house, where I dropped them off. I went home and spent the rest of my sleepless night collecting the various tools I would need to become the perfect cat burglar.

In the garage, I found a black Maglite flash-light and a long, heavy, nylon rope, one in which I could tie several knots in order to use as a climbing apparatus. I left the rope in the garage, but I took the flashlight, along with some fresh batteries, to my bedroom. Keep in mind that I was "spun out" on meth, meaning I created a complex chain of events out of what should have been a simple task. I decided that in addition to changing the batteries, I should clean the bulb and lens for optimum perfor-mance. I located and set aside an ensemble of black clothing, boots, and even a pair of Isotoner gloves in preparation for the night to come.

THE GRIP OF COCAINE

OUR CHRISTMAS BREAK ENDED AFTER that weekend, so it was back to school.

We resumed our normal activities and were especially relieved that there was no mention of anyone snooping around the school. We decided it best to keep this secret among the three of us; therefore, I couldn't tell KD—or anyone else, for that matter. The school week came to an end, the weekend arrived, and I was ready for another shot of meth.

I called KD and asked him if I could get three more quarters. He agreed he would try to find us some, but said that it might take a while. I waited patiently by the phone for several hours before he finally called me back. He told me to come pick him up so we could go get it. Instead of driving out into the country to the creepy trailer house, we went across town to an apartment complex. Once again, I waited in the car while he ran inside to get the stuff. After a few minutes, he emerged from the apartment, got in the car and we drove away. He pulled out the baggie before I could even ask him what it looked like. It appeared to be a larger quantity than the last one, so I asked him if he purchased the same amount. He explained that this bag was all powder instead of a rock but the weight was the same. It made sense to me and it seemed better that he wouldn't have to crush it in order to divide it. Once again he said he could not hang out with me that night because of other plans that he has already made.

We went back to his house, where he separated the dope, and then I left. I picked Buddy and JJ up later that evening and headed for the clinic. We rigged up the shots and fired them away, only this time, there was no rush or really much of anything accompanying it. The three of us walked all around the clinic, trying to convince ourselves that we were in fact wired. I couldn't imagine what was wrong with us, why it wasn't working this time. I mean, had we done something wrong? I was naïve enough to believe that every drug dealer was honest and all drugs were created equal.

Buddy said, "Let's get out of here. We're probably not feeling it because we're just sitting around inside this clinic doing nothing. Let's go find something to get into." His reasoning sounded logical, and I agreed being inside there was boring, so we headed for town. After riding around for a few hours and never feeling the effects we decided it probably wasn't us; not all dope was created equal, because this stuff was no good.

Angered by the lack of effects and embarrassed that I'd spent their money on something that was no good, I vowed to make it right as soon as possible. I dropped them off and returned home myself, disappointed at the outcome of the evening. The next day, I went to KD's to complain about the stuff. He agreed with me that it was no good, but he had been unsuccessful in contacting the guy he purchased it from. What a surprise!

KD looked at me and said, "That's the only problem with meth, man. You can't tell when you're buying it that it's going to be any good. Now, you see, coke, on the other hand, is easy to tell if it's real or not."

"What do you mean?" I asked.

He started explaining how even good meth can come in so many different colors, textures, smells, and tastes that it was virtually impossible to assess its value just by looking at it or tasting it, but that all cocaine had a similar taste and a very identifiable numbing effect. "Have you shot coke before?" I asked.

"Ohh, yeah; it's a much better rush than meth, and it's cheaper. For about a hundred dollars, you can get an eight ball of cocaine instead of just a gram." He must have known I was about to ask, because he told me that an eight ball was 3.5 grams, which was 1/8th of an ounce, hence the name.

"Do you know where to get some coke?" I asked.

"Big A does, but I haven't heard from him since that night we were all here."

I decided I was ready to go home and give up on the idea of getting high that weekend. I somehow knew we weren't going to get our money back, though KD said he was going to keep trying.

At the animal hospital, I worked with a girl named Lisa. Lisa was a rough- and-tough girl a couple of years older than me. She had attended my school and was considered very controversial because she was openly gay. As you can imagine, a proud lesbian attending a small town, she drew some attention. Once I started working with her, I was surprised to find she was really a nice person and wasn't nearly as rough and tough as she looked. I didn't know much about her, but I knew she regularly got high. As far as I knew, she only smoked weed, but I figured she might know someone who could find some coke. The next week at work, I finally worked up the courage to ask her. Much to my relief, she didn't give me a hard time for asking. In fact, she told me it would be no problem, that she could have it Friday. Though I had no idea of the effects of cocaine, I was excited as a five year old on Christmas morning. I felt very triumphant when telling KD that Friday evening, he and I would be driving to the next town to pick up and eight-ball of cocaine.

Friday night came, I picked up KD, and we headed off to meet Lisa. We drove about twenty-five miles to meet her at a truck stop. When we got there, she was waiting in her car. I got into her car to purchase the coke, and she told me she had taken out a little for putting the deal together. I was amazed at how large the rock was, so I didn't mind whatever she had removed. Remembering what KD had told me, before I got out of the car, I opened the baggie and tasted the contents. It had a strong medicinal, petroleum smell and that very identifiable numbing effect. I was satisfied that the stuff matched the trademarks KD had described, so I said, "Yeah, this tastes good—I appreciate it," and I got out of her car.

We drove from the truck stop to a friend's house to rig up a shot. I worked with another girl at the clinic, one with whom I was having an affair. She was nine years older than me, married, and had a house located about six miles south of town. I had been over to her house several times while her husband was at work, so I knew where the hidden key was. She and her husband were gone for the week on a vacation, and she had asked Lisa to take care of her dogs. I figured since she was gone, her house would be a safe place to shoot up.

I handed KD the bag of dope while I gathered a spoon and a glass of water and joined him at the kitchen table. I watched as he poured a fairly large amount onto the spoon, added 60 units of water, and started to stir the mixture. I was amazed at how much faster the cocaine dissolved than the meth. He pulled out a cigarette and bit a small piece off the butt. He dropped that piece into the faintly yellow, thick solution that was lying in the spoon. He drew up two shots, each of which contained just over 40 units of dope. He looked over at me and said, "Man, this is going to be a wild shot. I'll go first to make sure it's not too much for you."

I shot him up first and watched as he sprung from his chair and started walking around the kitchen, panting but not saying anything. His mouth was open, and he had a weird look like he had been really surprised all of a sudden. "Are you okay?" I kept asking, but he wouldn't answer me. He just kept panting and circling the kitchen. I stood up and started following him around, not sure if I should try to make him take a seat, throw some cold water on his face, or what to do. I had never seen an overdose but was starting to think he might be having one when he finally looked at me, grinned, and said, "Man, this is some good cocaine. You're going to love this."

Relieved and now excited, I quickly took a seat and started pumping up my left arm. He pulled up a chair in front of me, sat down, and grabbed the other rig. Still panting heavily, he gripped the syringe and tried to steady it directly over a large vein in the crease of my arm. In one solid motion, he stuck the needle in the vein, registered blood, and pushed the plunger home. As soon as he pulled the needle from my skin, I caught an unusual, ether-like taste in my mouth. Before I could even comment on it, what sounded like a freight train started running through my head. My heart started racing, and I felt as if I couldn't catch my breath. I sprung from my chair as I had seen KD do, but I couldn't circle the room because there was a deafening sound of *womp, womp, womp* cycling through my head—and everything in sight was shaking. I could feel my body involuntarily shaking from side to side, and I was unsure my legs could support my body.

For fear of falling, I quickly took a seat on the floor, trying to ride this thing out. After about a minute or so, the shaking stopped, and the freight train sound was replaced by KD's voice asking if I was okay. Once I realized I was fine, I joined him in praising this newfound friend called cocaine. "Man, you were right. This is way better than meth," I told him as I started trying to pick up our mess. Though I knew the owners of the house were supposed to be gone for a few more nights, I suddenly became nervous, thinking, *What if they decided to come home a few days early, and here we are, shooting coke in their kitchen?*

We quickly cleaned up our mess and left the house without a trace. We drove to town in search of some action, but as usual, found none. After an hour or so of riding around, KD said that we should go over to Deena's house. Deena was a girl who had graduated the year before and gone off to college but was home for the Christmas break. Apparently, she and KD had been seeing each other for a while, because he knew she would more than welcome us into her home with an eight ball of cocaine.

She was a very pretty, popular girl in high school, so I was excited to go and get high with her. KD told me she was unaware of him shooting up, so I was not to mention it, and that we should be snorting a line or two with her. We arrived at her house, snorted a few lines, and spent the rest of the evening rambling on about absolutely nothing. My 1:00 a.m. curfew arrived, and I knew I had to get home. I wanted to go home and then sneak back out in order to keep partying.

KD said that he and Deena would come pick me up at the store that was close by my house and 1:30 a.m. He suggested I leave the coke with them instead of risking driving around with it. It sounded like a good idea to me, since they were going to come and get me anyway.

Well, as you can imagine, they never showed up for answered the phone. To ensure that I wouldn't take the car out once I got home, my father required me to relinquish the keys at night, and before this night, it had not occurred to me to make a duplicate set. While waiting at the store, I discovered the major difference between a cocaine high and a meth high—the come down. I felt as if one minute I was speeding and ready to go; then suddenly, I was wearing a suit made out of lead. This was my first encounter with "jonesing," so all I could think of was how much I needed another shot of coke.

I waited at the store until 2:00 a.m. before I headed home on the walk of shame. I snuck back into my house, resentfully called it a night, and laid in bed until I fell asleep. The next day, I drove to Deena's house to get my coke and see what kind of excuse they would come up with. KD gave me some crazy excuse that Deena's father came home, so he'd had to hide in her closet for about an hour while she pretended to be sleeping; they'd been unable to come and get me or even answer the phone. I really wanted to believe him and almost did until he presented the tiny rock that was the remains of my eight ball.

"Dude, what happened to it?" I asked as he handed me the baggie. It appeared to be only half the size it had been the night before. He started reminding me of how much we had done the night before and swore that he and Deena had not done any of it without me. Though I knew he was lying, I couldn't prove it, so I decided it best to take the remaining coke and leave without making any unsupported accusations. I went home to call Buddy and JJ to tell them I had their money's worth of some good dope. Neither of them was doing anything important at the time, so they both agreed that a shot of cocaine sounded good.

It was mid-afternoon before I showered, changed, and left my house to get them. I was supposed to work alone at the clinic that afternoon, so I knew we could safely rig up our shots without drawing suspicion from my car being parked outside. Once inside, I started gathering the necessary items in order to rig up the shots. I fixed the rigs, administered the shots, and proudly watched as the

rush swept over them. "I told you it was good, didn't
I?" I said as I watched them panting and circling
the room. Though this was only my second shot to
do, I acted as if I knew all about this stuff and they
should be thankful I'd introduced them to it.

I can now honestly say that never could my
thinking have been more polluted. I hate the fact
I allowed the enemy to use me in order to spread
destruction into the lives of two of my friends, but
as any addict will tell you, drugs never seem bad
at first.

As I hoped, they praised me for scoring something that made them feel so good, but unlike me,
they didn't seem to mind the come down as much.
I, on the other hand, wanted to do shot after shot.
I never wanted to come down. We spent the next
few hours doing blasts before they decided they'd
have enough and were ready to go home. I was kind
of relieved at their decision, because I really didn't
want to share any more of my cocaine. I dropped
them off, returned to the clinic, and spent the rest
of the evening alone, shooting up the remainder of
the eight ball. I stayed at the clinic peering out the
window to make sure no one was going to surprise
me by walking in unannounced. When I ran out
of coke, I sat there and jonesed for a while before I
decided I better call it a night and go home.

During my two-week crash course on shooting drugs, I found only one thing wrong with
them—they were very expensive. My mind started
racing through ideas on ways to make money but

I couldn't find one that would apply to me. Buying that eight ball depleted my funds, and it would be another two weeks before I got paid again. KD told me of a way to get high smoking banana peels. He claimed that I could cook the peels in a microwave until they were completely dried of all moisture, tear them into small pieces, roll it up, and smoke it. After school one afternoon, I tried it but did not get high, so I called him to see if he would come to my house to show me what I was doing wrong. He agreed to come, so I headed over to pick him up. We got to my house, and for about an hour, we unsuccessfully attempted to get high using bananas. We were standing in my garage trying to smoke the second banana joint when KD noticed several cans of Rustoleum brand spray paint.

"Oh, man, do you know what will give you a good buzz?" he asked with a large, devilish grin on his face.

Puzzled, wondering what other crazy idea he had come up with, I said, "No, I can't imagine."

"Paint," he said. "What?"

"Huffing, paint, dude. You spray paint into the opening of a bread bag, put the opening over your mouth and nose, and start inhaling the fumes."

As he was giving me these instructions, I remembered hearing about the possibilities of getting high from the fumes of things like paint, gas, or even liquid paper. This, to me, definitely sounded like a much better idea than the whole banana thing, so inside we went to get a bread bag. I retrieved a bag, and we returned to the garage, where KD grabbed a full can of black paint. I watched as he sprayed several large shots of paint into the bag, put it to his mouth, and started breathing in the fumes. After about four large gulps from the bag, he pinched it closed and handed it to me. He started laughing as he moved to sit down, telling me to add some more paint to the bag. Not certain of how much to add, but sure I wanted to catch a good buzz, I loaded the bag up and started inhaling anyway. KD was off in another world, so he couldn't tell me I had sprayed in too much and I was taking in too many gulps of air. After about ten large gulps, I took a seat on the deep freeze, and the room started rocking.

The next thing I knew, I had somehow moved out onto the grass in the front yard. It was a beautiful day. The sky was clear and appeared to be a deeper blue than I had ever seen. There was a slight, cool breeze blowing from the north, but it wasn't powerful enough to shadow the warming effects of the bright sun. I was sitting on the well-manicured lawn, running my hands across the cool green grass, when I heard a loud rumble from above. I looked up, and to my surprise, I saw an enormous hand reaching down from the heavens toward me. Though the hand seemed to take up most of the sky, I was not afraid.

"Oh, wow, man," is all I could say as I curiously watched the giant hand moving in. Then suddenly, for no particular reason, my surroundings changed. Instead of sitting in the grass on my front lawn, I was now standing outside the world, gazing in. Then I realized it was *my* hand reaching down through the sky at my tiny self sitting in the grass staring back at me. If that wasn't tripped out enough, I heard another rumble coming from behind me. My surroundings changed again; now I was sitting in an oversized, brown leather recliner and staring at a television the size of a movie theater screen. At first, there was nothing but the static on the monitor; then it started clearing. I strained to see the images emerging from the static as my chair seemed to magically move toward the large screen. My focus adjusted, and I was able to see myself standing outside the world, reaching down through the clouds toward myself sitting in the front yard of my father's lawn. Just as I was thinking, *Man, this is cool,* I woke up and realized I was still sitting on the freezer inside the garage.

I was so disappointed when I realized it was all just a hallucination. I say hallucination, but it was more like astral projection, which makes me wonder about the mindset of those who claim they had an out-of-body experience. While I was tripping on acid, I saw things change their appearance, but nothing like this. I would say this wicked trip was something like when the Indians ate peyote and took a journey into the spirit world. I really wanted to try it again, but my head felt strange and my stomach started feeling queasy. I thought it best for me to go and lie down in my bed. I intended on getting back up in a short while to make sure the paint cans were put away and all incriminating evidence was disposed of, but that didn't happen.

KD left shortly after I passed out for fear of my parents coming home and finding only him awake. He told me later how he tried several times to wake me up but couldn't seem to get my attention. I finally did wake up to my father shaking me and asking what was wrong with me and why was there such a strong smell of paint in the house. Apparently, when I came inside from the closed garage, I left the door open. As my father left the bedroom to investigate the smell, I remembered the bag I left lying on the garage floor and the paint cans that were still sitting on the deep freeze. I knew I was busted, so I decided it was best to remain incoherent in order to avoid having to answer some very difficult questions.

As I expected, he came charging back into my room with a paint-filled bread bag, wanting some sort of explanation. I stuck to my guns and pretended to be in such an inebriated state that I was unaware of his efforts to wake me. He started rummaging through my stuff. I knew what he was doing, but I also knew I could do nothing to stop him; so I laid there praying he didn't find my jean jacket. After a couple of minutes of him digging through my pockets of various articles of clothing, he suddenly got quiet, and I knew why.

He found my stash of three syringes I had hidden inside the pockets of my blue jean jacket. "Carl, are these your needles?" he asked, alarmed. I did not answer or in any way let on that I understood the question. He decided it was best to wait until I woke up to obtain an answer, so he left the room. I remained there, lying in bed until I came up with what I thought might be a plausible explanation. I told him the stuff belonged to KD, that he had borrowed my jean jacket about a week prior, and by accident had left it here today. My father didn't believe me, though I swore it was the truth.

The next week, he scheduled an evening appointment with a drug counselor, and I had to go. I met with the counselor and started telling him that I never shot up any type of drugs and that I didn't even smoke weed anymore. He listened intently, and for a moment, I thought I had convinced him of my innocence—until he asked me for a urine sample.

My stomach dropped when he insisted on the sample, because I had smoke weed earlier that day. I thought about rescinding my statement but decided against it. I'd wait for the results of the screen before I started telling him of all the different drugs I had done. I mean, there was no sense admitting to doing something unless I had to. My father and I left the office and quietly drove home. The counselor told my father that each of his and my sessions would be kept anonymous and that my father shouldn't pry. He told my father if I wanted him to know something about our sessions I would volunteer the information. My father respected the boundaries the counselor established and did not

ask me a single question about my session, though
I know he wanted to. I know he desperately wanted
to know how to help his son.

The next day, as soon as I left school, I went to
the hardware store and made a copy of my car key.
I knew my father would be receiving a phone call
soon and that I would definitely lose the keys to the
car. I walked on eggshells the entire evening, thinking every time the phone rang it was the counselor.
Nothing happened that evening, so I started thinking maybe I had somehow miraculously passed the
drug screen.

The next day, however, I wasn't so lucky. My
father came home with news that the test results
showed my system to contain a high level of THC
and a moderate level of cocaine. Though I knew I
was going to be faced with some questions, I was
not prepared to with any answers. I admitted to
smoking the weed and told him I had snorted some
coke the prior weekend, but I stuck to my story
about the syringes. I know he wanted to believe
that was true, but I could tell his better judgment
kept that from happening. He told me of a series of
appointments he made with the counselor and how
much he loved me and just wanted to help.

Those words burnt into me like hot lead, and
for a moment, I felt as if I wanted to break down
and cry. It was as if there were two voices inside
my head, one telling me to get off this road I had
started down, the other enticing me forward. I
didn't break down and cry though. And, of the two

voices, I listened to the one telling me, *Oh, man, everything is going to be all right. The drugs aren't the problem. You were just careless and got caught. Now, you just need to ride this thing out and win back everyone's trust*

———◆◆◆◆———

"That's right, Carl. It's not that you can't handle the dope." Nakot slowly circled around the teenager. "You've just got to slow down a little, and be a lot more careful. You'll get everybody's trust back. Just be smart and tell them what they want to hear."

Kansra chuckled to himself as he started to slowly clap. "Well, Nakot, you seem to have your challenge going in the right direction."

"Ah, thank you, sire," replied Nakot. "I sure am enjoying this."

"You fool!" roared Kansra. "This job is not for your enjoyment. You are on a results-oriented mission. Until his soul is ours, there is no victory. Do you understand me?"

"Yes, sire, I understand."

"Good," said Kansra as he lowered his voice. "You're going to have to convince him he's in control. Keep him focused on the need to stay high. Don't allow him to recognize the damage he's doing to his parents."

"Well, how do I keep him from recognizing that?"

"I just told you, you idiot," barked Kansra. "By keeping him focused on the need to stay high. Nakot, your challenge is an addict. Half your battle is already won. If you play this right, you'll be able to destroy his life and the lives of all those around him. Addicts are like tornadoes. They suck in everyone they can and rip them apart. If it weren't for the disgust and sheer hatred I have for humans, I would consider addicts allies."

Nakot sat there nodding his head. "Yes, yes, I know what you mean, sire." "Stay focused and be relentless," ordered Kansra as he turned to leave.

"You better not disappoint me."

"I won't, sire," Nakot replied. "You'll see, I'll get him."

THE VAULT

AS I SUSPECTED, MY DAD TOLD ME I could use the car only to travel to and from school. Surprisingly, he was nice about the situation. "Carl, if you were driving around high, got into a wreck, and hurt someone, they could sue me and my company, since the car is in my name." What he told me made sense, and to say the least, I couldn't blame him for his concerns. For the next few weeks, I calmed down considerably. I knew the best way to get my car back and to step out of the spotlight I had pointed on my life was to walk the line and make some headway with the drug counselor.

I only had to meet with the counselor once a week, and I knew if I spent the hour telling him what I thought he wanted to hear, I could escape with minimal confrontation. Though I don't think he entirely believed me, he reported to my father that our sessions were going well and I seemed honest in wanting to get help. Nothing could have been further from the truth. February 7, 1988, was a Sunday. I still couldn't use the car for anything outside traveling to and from school, and hanging out with KD was no longer something I could tell my father I was doing. But, when KD called and told me he had some meth, I quickly devised a scheme, which involved KD's younger sister, Janet.

Janet was a sophomore in high school, and for a few years now, I had known of the tremendous crush she had on me. I knew she would have no problem coming to pick me up and taking me out to meet KD and Deena at Deena's father's hunting lodge. Janet picked me up around 7:00 p.m. We arrived at the lodge, where I quickly joined KD in the bathroom to do a much needed shot. I don't know if Deena and Janet knew what we were doing, but neither said anything to us when we came walking out wired up and ready to go.

KD found a bottle of tequila in a cabinet behind a wet bar. With Deena's approval, he grabbed a couple of shot glasses and headed to the kitchen area to set up at the table. The four of us started playing quarters, using a shot of tequila instead of a glass of beer as the penalty for a miss. As you can imagine, it was a short-lived game. The girls got really drunk, but KD and I were something else.

This was only my third time to shoot speed, and this was the first time I mixed it with large amounts of alcohol. I found that, as usual, I was wired for sound and ready to go, but for the first time, I had no inhibitions. I felt completely fearless.

Because it was a school night and we each needed to get home at a reasonable hour, we decided to call it a night around 11:00p.m. On the drive home, I couldn't help but notice the abnormally heavy fog bank that seemed to envelope the town. As I arrived at my house and stepped from the car, I noticed the house two lots down was no longer visible. I told Janet good night and proceeded inside, making just enough noise to let my father know I had safely returned home.

I went to the bedroom, closed and locked the door, and started preparing for the "crime of the century." I knew the fog would prohibit anyone from seeing the school while passing by on the road, and traffic would be minimal at best because it was late Sunday night. I decided to wait for a while in order to allow ample time for my father to fall back asleep. After about an hour, I got out of bed, donned the all-black clothing, boots, and gloves I had set aside, picked up my flashlight, and quietly headed for the garage. I removed the lineman's rope from a hook on the wall, grabbed a framing hammer and a towel, and slipped out the front door without making a sound. I used the copied key to open the car, put it in neutral, and quietly pushed it down the street. After about a hundred yards, I jumped in, cranked it, and headed off toward the school.

While driving by, I could see there was no part of the school building that could be seen from the road. I then felt more confident in my plan, so I headed to JJ's house to wake him. Of the three of us, Buddy was the least interested in my plot to rob the vault; therefore, I decided against involving him. I arrived in JJ's neighborhood and parked along the street a few houses down from his. I quickly ran to his bedroom window and started lightly tapping on the glass. His parent's bedroom was right next to his, and I could hear his father snoring through their window. I tapped and tapped on the glass but got no response. I decided it was useless and I had better leave when I heard his father abruptly stop snoring. I ran back to my car and pulled away from there, thinking, *Oh, well, you don't need him. You don't need anybody. Let's get this thing done.*

Any voice of reason in my mind was drowned out by the alluring thoughts of what I could do with all that money. I pulled down the same side street as before, except this time, I followed it to the end. The street dead-ended into that same large, overgrown field we had passed through on my first visit. At the end of the street, I noticed a four wheeler trail that seemed to disappear into the tall grass. I pulled my small car down the trail until I was convinced it could not be seen by anyone from anywhere. I exited the car, ran across the fields, and slipped up behind the principal's office window. A chair rail sash divided the large window into two parts, the bottom of which was about four feet wide and four feet high and started at ground level. I placed the folded towel in the center of the bottom portion of the window and swung the hammer hard. The hammer and towel successfully broke through the glass, creating only a small amount of noise. The window was made of safety glass, which kept it from breaking into large, dangerous shards and allowed for easier removal.

I quickly made a large enough hole to slip in and out and crawled through. I walked through the principal's office, across the front of the vault, and into JJ's mother's office. I climbed on top of the chair, removed the ceiling tiles, and tied the rope to a secure structure above. Before trying climbing knots in the rope, I decided to take a look through the hole in the vault wall. I was hoping I could see well enough inside the vault to determine if I would need a rope. I pulled out my flashlight and started trying to pull my way up into the hole. I quickly realized the hole was too high and not large enough for me to go through on my stomach. I would have to pull myself up by the piping above and use the pipes to pull my way through the hole and into the vault. For fear I might not be able to easily pull my way back out of the opening, I decided to tie several climbing knots in the rope, push it through, turn on my flashlight, and go for it.

The hole was smaller than I thought, and even though I changed my mode of entry, it was still very difficult to pull my way through. At the point I was about halfway through the wall, I accidentally dropped my flashlight. It fell about two feet before it crashed onto the grid that held the tiles that covered the ceiling of the vault. The light immediately extinguished, and I heard the gut-wrenching sound of the batteries ejecting from the flashlight. I was now in absolute darkness, and though I tried desperately to locate the components of the light, I finally conceded it was useless and crawled out of the hole.

I remembered JJ suggesting the chemistry lab as a probable source for locating a flashlight, so I took my hammer, left the office, and headed down the hall. I knew each classroom door was locked, but conveniently, there was a thin window running up the top half of the door, located just to the right of the turn knob. I arrived at the lab door and, without hesitation, used the hammer to break through the window. I then reached through, turned the knob from the inside, and opened the door.

I turned on the light and quickly started rummaging through the drawers and storage closets in search of a much-needed flashlight. Much to my disappointment, I could not find a flashlight, but I did locate some candles and a cigarette lighter I figured would probably work. I grabbed two of the large white candles and headed back down the hallway. Inside the office, I climbed back onto the chair, and with the candle in hand, I reached through the hole in the wall. I lodged the candle on top of the piping inside the vault, placed the lighter between my teeth, and commenced to squeeze my way back through the opening. At the halfway point, I removed the candle from the piping above, took the lighter from my mouth, lit the candle, and started looking for the various components of my flashlight. I found all the missing parts except for the clear lens that protects the bulb. This was a part I could live without, and because I had already wasted a lot of precious time on my venture to the chemistry lab, I decided to go on without it. I reassembled then turned on the light, blew out the candle, and finished pulling my way into the vault.

I kept a firm grip on the piping above, which now supported all my weight. In one solid motion, I pulled my feet from the hole, causing the lower half of my body to fall and take out a portion of the suspended ceiling. I let go of the pipes, dropped through the opening I made, and successfully landed in the middle of the vault. Using the flashlight, I started looking around the small room. I quickly located the light switch, turned it on, and assessed my surroundings.

Much to my relief, I learned I could open the vault door from the inside, meaning I wouldn't have to scale back out with the loot. I opened the door a little, so as not to let too much light escape, turned, and started looking for the money. I found several cigar boxes filled with cash. Attached to some of the cash were small notes with student's names written on them or classrooms that it came from. There were several bank bags filled with various dollar amounts. I decided it was not the time to count, so I grabbed two of the larger bags and completely filled them before turning for the door. At the base of the door, on the right-hand side, I noticed two large drawstring-type money bags filled with loose quarters. I knew this must be a collection from every vending machine on the campus, and now that collection belonged to me. I tucked the cash-filled bank bags inside the waist of my jeans, picked up the two heavy bags of quarters, and exited the vault.

I removed my rope, grabbed my hammer, towel, and bags, and headed back out through the broken window. I was relieved to find the heavy fog bank was still lingering. I ran through the cover of fog, across the fields to my car. I quickly jumped into my car, dropped the money bags into the rear passenger floorboard, cranked it, and drove away. The short drive home seemed longer than ever before, though I gained more confidence in my clean escape with each passing mile.

When I got to my street, I put the car in neutral, killed the engine, and coasted to a stop in front of my house. I quietly ran from the car to the garage, where I re-hung the rope and grabbed a shovel. I left the garage, grabbed the two satchels of quarters, and walked into an overgrown field beside the house. In the field stood a large, old oak tree surrounded by a cover of tall grass. At the base of the tree, I dug a deep hole, dropped the bags of quarters, and covered them with dirt. I returned to the house, placed the shovel in the garage, and quietly slipped back into my room. For fear I might have woken someone, I quickly shed my clothing and placed it, along with the bags of cash, into the closet. I got into bed, pretending to be asleep, while listening for the sounds my father would make if he were coming to check on me. After about twenty minutes of lying there, I realized I had pulled it off and my father was not going to barge through the door.

I got out of bed, removed the cash from the money-bags, and started placing it inside the pockets of shirts and jackets that hung in the closet. I placed my soiled clothing in the dirty clothes hamper and got back into bed. I laid there the remainder of the night fantasizing about what I was going to do with my small fortune. To make sure that no one walked in on me while counting, I decided to leave the money uncounted until the next day after school.

The next morning, I was up and stirring earlier than normal. I showered, put on much nicer clothing than I normally wore to school, and headed out the door. As suspected, I saw several police cars sitting outside the front of the school as I drove to the back to park my car. As I was walking across the lawn toward the entrance of the school, I saw Buddy and JJ coming out to greet me. As they approved, I couldn't help but notice the large grins on their faces, as if they were silently seeking some sort of acknowledgement of me being responsible for the caper.

"Dude, someone beat us to it," Buddy naively said.

"No kidding?" I replied, without asking what he was referring to.

JJ picked up on it and said, "You did it, didn't you?" Though I had decided it was best to tell no one of my guilt, I was vainly proud of my accomplishment and wanted them to know I had pulled it off. I told them I had done it and, though I had not counted it, knew it was a considerable amount of money.

"Man, why didn't you come get me?" asked JJ. I told him of my futile attempt to wake him and then deciding the night was too perfect to let it pass. I told them we had to act as shocked and appalled as everyone else and under no circumstances were they to tell anyone. They agreed, the bell rang, and off to class we went.

I couldn't help but smile as I passed several groups of students discussing their theories on who was responsible for this dastardly deed. I even participated with other students in acting offended, as if this vile act had in some way violated us. The school day ended, and I rushed home to count my loot. I knew I would be alone at the house for about two hours before my father got off work. That would give me enough time to count the money and get the ball rolling on purchasing an ounce of cocaine. As I started pulling the money from various pockets, I was amazed at the amount of ten and twenty-dollar bills that were mixed up with the expected ones. After counting it twice, I was satisfied that $1,786 was the total of cash, and I still had two large bags of loose quarters, which I estimated to be around $400. "Score," I yelled. "Man, I've got enough money for an ounce of coke, an ounce of weed, and still have party money left over."

I put all but $200 of the money back into the pockets of my clothing and sat down to call Lisa. A bit set off by the amount I was asking for, she told me to give her a little time to try to put the order together. I told her I was about to leave my house, but that I'd page her when I got back home. I scooped up the $200 and headed out the door toward KD's house to buy an ounce of weed. When I got there, he told me he only had a half ounce left, so I agreed to purchase that and wait on him to "re-up." I told him I couldn't stay long, but that I'd burn a joint with him. We got high and talked about how shocked we were that someone had boldly broken into the school and made off with what he heard was around $5,000. It's funny how inflated numbers get when people start speculating about events such as that. I left there shortly after finishing the joint for fear that if I remained much longer, I might reveal too much information. Though I thought I could probably trust KD, I decided it was best not to tell him I was responsible.

I returned home to page Lisa in hopes she had located an ounce of coke for me to purchase. After about an hour, she called back to tell me I would have to wait until Friday to purchase the ounce, that her guy was out of town and wouldn't be back until then. Because I had been going for almost thirty-six hours with no sleep, I decided to call it a night rather early and get some much-needed rest.

Tuesday morning arrived, and I sprang from the bed to head off to school. I was in an optimistic, giddy state of mind. I was convinced I would become a very prosperous, well-respected drug dealer, starting with just one ounce of coke. I arrived at school and went to class as normal. There were no police cars at the school; in fact, the buzz from the previous day seemed to have ended. It was second period, shortly after 9:00a.m., when a secretary called the classroom requesting my presence in the office. She said they were having trouble with my new class schedule. I didn't think much of this because I had made a class schedule change a few weeks prior.

I left the classroom and started my journey down the hallway. To get to the office, I had to exit the main hallway and walk down a smaller hallway that led only into the office. When I stepped into the smaller hallway, I could see through the glass door that there were two detective standing in front of the office waiting for me. They saw me as quickly as I saw them, and one of them gave me a large, suspicious grin. To put it mildly, my stomach dropped, my heart started racing, and I thought, *Oh God, please don't let this be happening.* I knew if I tried to turn back, I would really look guilty—as if my sudden uncontrollable shaking wasn't obvious enough. I walked through the door and said, "Hello" as I passed them on my way to the front counter. Trying to remain calm, as I would if I were not guilty, I looked at the secretary and said, "Ma'am, you called for me."

She appeared to be as nervous as I was when she started to talk. She found herself speechless in trying to answer my question. Instead, she looked from me to the detectives and said, "What do you want to do?"

I felt my world close in when I heard the older of the two detectives ask if "we" could use the vice principal's office. With her approval, he then turned to me and said, "Carl, let's go have a talk."

It was all I could do to place one foot in front of the other and walk my way back to that office. I walked into the office, and as instructed, I took a seat in front of the desk. The older detective sat behind the desk while the younger one pulled a chair up next to me.

"Carl, what do you think we could possibly be here for?" asked the older detective.

I had stolen a "get out of class" pass booklet from the office the first time Buddy, JJ, and I snuck into the school. I learned that if I waited until the roll call was turned in from third period, I could write myself out of class; then the office would not know that I had left. If I was present through roll call of the third period, then I was considered present for the entire day, because no other roll calls were turned into the office. Using this pad, I had written myself out of class five times in the past few weeks. I knew that by law I was required to attend school, so I replied, "Is this about me skipping school?"

The younger of the two officers started to chuckle, but the older one didn't find humor in my ridiculous response. "No, Carl, we're not here because you've skipped some classes. Why don't you tell me what you did Sunday night." Remembering that I had to exude innocence, I confidently but respectfully started telling them of my night with KD and friends, which ended around 11:00 p.m.

The younger of the two said, "Carl, why don't you tell us what you did after they dropped you off, and who was with you when you did it."

"I-I-I don't know what you're talking about, sir," I sheepishly replied.

The older of the two lost his patience. "Look here, Mr. Miller, we're not up here wasting our time to listen to some stupid story about you skipping school.

We know what you did Sunday night and that you weren't alone. Now, I don't know who you are trying to protect, but lying to us is only going to make things worse."

Because they seemed to be very adamant about knowing I was responsible, I immediately thought of the lost lens in my flashlight. I was not wearing gloves the night I disassembled it for cleaning. I figured they must have found the lens and retrieved my fingerprints from it.

I sat there silently looking at the floor, processing all the different variables when the older detective calmly said, "Look, Carl, we know you broke into the school and stole the money. What we can't figure out is why. I mean, you are a good kid, from a well-respected family, who was just awarded the Outstanding High School Students of America Award. Why would you want to jeopardize your future by breaking into the school?"

I did not respond or even look up until I heard the younger cop say,

"Because you're shooting up coke now, aren't you?"

Shocked by his knowledge of what I'd been doing, I started to think I was truly busted and there was no lying my way out of it.

"Look at me, son." I looked across the desk at the older officer. "Now stop making it harder on yourself and tell us who you did this with. We don't believe you were the mastermind behind this thing, so tell us who influenced you to do it."

Convinced that they found the lens, which would prove I was there, I finally gave up my defense and said, "There was no one with me." The older detective grinned and nodded his head as if he had won a great victory. The younger of the two started drilling me again about who was with me because neither of them believed I was capable of performing a feat like that alone. I continued trying to convince them I acted alone and there was truly no outside influence spawning my decision. I'm not sure they ever entirely believed me, but they quit drilling me once I explained, in detail, how I gained entry into the vault. They told me it would be better for me if I returned the money; so I agreed to take a ride with them to my house to retrieve it.

On the way to my house, they asked me how I got started doing coke. They told me I could help myself get out of some of this trouble if I was willing to cooperate with them.

"What do you mean 'cooperate'?" I asked.

The younger detective looked back from the front passenger seat. "Well, Carl, we know you're a small fish. Now, if you provide us with information about some big fish, then you might walk away from this without going to prison."

Not going to prison sounded like a great thing. The only problem was I didn't know any "big fish." *Maybe I could by some time by playing along and pretending to know some cartel-type guys.* I started telling them I got my stuff from a heavy hitter, a gangbanger, who lived in the city about twenty-five miles away. We arrived at my house, and the older cop turned to look at me. "Carl, if you'll provide us with some names and help set up a buy or two with one of our undercover guys tagging along, we'll go to bat for you with the judge."

"What does that mean, 'go to bat for me with the judge'?" I asked. "We can't tell you the outcome of the charges that will be filed against you—only the judge can make that decision. What I'm telling you is that my recommendation to the judge carries a lot of weight. If you work with us, we'll work with you."

I told them I would help them catch this fictitious gangbanger I invented, but I was concerned about the safety of me and my family.

The older cop said, "I tell you what we're going to do. Let's go inside and get this money, and then we'll take you back to the school. No one knows you're with us right now; so you can go back to class, finish the day, and come down to the police station after school to turn yourself in. Now, Carl, it's very important that you come to the station right after you get out of school. Do you understand?"

You betcha, I thought as I replied, "yes, sir, I understand, and I'll be there by four p.m."

Satisfied I would keep up my end of the bargain, the three of us made a pact that I was going to secretly work for them. We left the car, went inside, and I started removing the cash from my clothes. I retrieved all but one pile of cash and handed it to them, stating that was all I had. Apparently, they had no idea how much money was missing, because they didn't question the amount I gave them. I volunteered the location of the two bags of quarters; I could tell by their expressions they were unaware the quarters were even missing.

We returned to the car, where they put the cash into an evidence bag.

They then put the bag along with the two satchels of quarters into the trunk. As promised, we returned to the school, where they dropped me off out front. It was the middle of third period, around 10:30 a.m., when I stepped from the car and heard the older officer say, "Now, Carl, make sure you come directly to the station after school. Got it?"

"Yes, sir. I got it. I'll be there," I replied as I closed the car door and walked toward the front door of the school. As I approached the front door, I watched in the reflection of the windows as the detective's car drove away. Once inside the door, I turned to watch them pull off the campus drive and disappear down the street. I then turned and started briskly walking down the long hallway toward the back of the school. The reality of the whole situation hit me, and all I could think about was not going to prison. I was heading back for the back parking lot to get my car when I heard the principal calling my name. I looked back to see him waving and trying to catch up with me. I ignored his attempts to stop me as I left the building, got into my car, and drove away. It became clear what I had to do. In fact, it was the only logical thing to do. I had to escape to Mexico. *I'll go to Boys' Town,* I thought. I had no idea where "Boys' Town" was, but I heard it was an anything-goes kind of place located somewhere around Juarez,Mexico.

I sped home to gather some things I knew I would need in order to make the journey. I arrived at my house, ran inside, and started packing luggage bags with clothing, hygiene products, canned foods, my weed, money, my father's.357 Magnum pistol, and around a hundred shells. I loaded all the bags into my car and cranked the engine. I realized I had no idea how to get to Mexico, so I went back inside to find a road atlas. A large United States Road Atlas had been on the coffee table in my father's living room for several months. The atlas was part of an array of magazines that were used as decorations for the centerpiece of the table. Though I remembered seeing the atlas on the table within the last few weeks, now, when I suddenly needed it, it was nowhere in sight. I frantically searched through the magazines three times before I conceded to the fact that it just wasn't there. I took my search from the table to the bottom cabinets of a large wall piece. The cabinets were filled with an assortment of various types of magazines. I searched through the cabinets thoroughly but could not find the atlas. I somehow knew the only way my escape was going to be a success was if I got out of town quickly. I remember thinking I really had to hurry because the police would be patrolling the borders, as if I was a dangerous terrorist fleeing the government.

I left the living room in a freaked out state of mind and headed for my father's bedroom closet. I rummaged through the closet but still found nothing in the way of a map. It finally occurred to me to stop and purchase an atlas once I had safely arrived in a larger town. On my way out of the house, I gave one last glance into the cabinets in the living room. I don't know how I missed it, but right there on top, underneath one magazine, was the atlas. Relieved, I smiled and said, "There it is, you big dummy. How did you miss that?" I grabbed the atlas and headed out the door. As I passed through the doorway, I saw my father's truck pull in the driveway.

I could feel my world closing in as he exited his truck, saying, "Carl, is it true? Did you do it?" I could think of nothing to say in response to his question as I lowered my head and started to cry.

———————•◆•———————

"Ahh," cried Nakot, "I was so close. Boy, if I could have gotten you to Mexico, this pursuit would have ended quickly."

"Close, huh," commented Kansra as he suddenly appeared behind Nakot. "Kansra, I mean, sire!" exclaimed Nakot. "Did you see how close I was? I had him convinced to flee to Mexico. But, out of nowhere, the Christ-following father showed up and ruined my plans. Now I see why you call these relatives of Christian's challenges."

"I told you," said Kansra. "In fact, things are about to get even more challenging. The boy's in trouble now, and will probably be sent away. Use this to your advantage. Work your persuasion into the minds of those he comes in contact with. Convince him to move away from his God-fearing parents to minimize all contact with them. We have to get him away from the truth his family is trying to provide. You're going to have to orchestrate something to keep him from accepting responsibility for his actions. If he starts to think he has a problem, he may start seeking the only real solution. Do not let that happen!"

DODGING PRISON

MY REACTION TO HIS QUESTION brought tears to his eyes as the cold realization set in that his son was in a real bind. My father called an attorney, who asked me a series of questions about my interview with the police. As I later found out, they didn't really have anything on me until I confessed. They found JJ's prints on the desk drawers of the principal's office. There was no way for JJ to go through the principal's desk during normal office hours, so the police figured he had been there after hours. The police went to him; despite the fact we had been good friends for three years, when asked, he simply said, "No, I didn't do it. Carl did." When the police came to visit me, all they had on me was hearsay, which would not have been enough for a conviction. They kept telling me they knew I had done it and that by not cooperating with them, I was only making things worse for myself. What they did not say was that I was under arrest and had the right to an attorney.

When my attorney questioned them about this, they simply replied, "Well, heck, Russell. He could have got up and left that office whenever he wanted. We never told him he couldn't leave." I felt disgusted when I was slapped in the face with this reality. My attorney, Russell, made arrangements with the DA to allow me to go to a drug rehabilitation hospital that night. I was court-ordered to stay in that lockdown juvenile rehab until I successfully completed the program. At that point, I would return to the courts for the trial. My father drove me to the police station, where I was booked for "burglary of a building." I bonded out, went to the DA's office, signed some paperwork, and headed off to the rehab hospital. I was afraid of going off to a strange hospital to live, but at the same time, I was relieved to be leaving town without having to see anyone or answer any questions.

I arrived at the hospital and took the elevator to the fifth floor. The entire fifth floor of this Humana Hospital was designated for chemical dependency and psychological disorders. When the elevator stopped and the doors opened, the first thing I saw through the thick window of door in front of me was several older people with wild, messy hair. They were dressed only in hospital gowns and appeared to be walking aimlessly throughout the hallway. I began to think,

Maybe prison won't be so bad, as I watched the people roaming around without purpose.

My dad could see the apprehension I was expressing and said, "That's the psyche ward, Carl. It looks like the door we want is around the corner." Sure enough, I saw the signs stating that that half of the fifth floor was the Psychiatric Ward and the other half, my half, was around the corner. We reached the large, heavy, secured door that was the entrance to my new home. No one but the patients could be allowed inside, so I had to say my tear-filled good-byes at the door.

The clothes I had originally packed for my trip to Mexico now became my wardrobe for the next several months. I was only one of three eighteen-year-olds admitted into this juvenile facility. Most eighteen-year-olds were sent to an adult facility, but because we were still actively pursuing a high school diploma, we were allowed to stay. The other thirty or so students ranged in ages from fourteen to seventeen years old. We all had a common problem: we liked acting out and getting high. The program consisted of four levels of completion, all of which were required for graduation from the facility. I was concerned when I found out the earliest anyone had graduated from the program was four months. I was disgusted when I found out there were three students present that had been there for over a year and were still on level three.

It was rough at first, but as with anything, once I adjusted, it became normal. The curriculum at the facility's school was considered at a special- education level. The majority of the students needed this level of education in order to stand a chance of understanding the material. I only needed to finish my History and English 4 in order to graduate from high school. Because of the substandard level, I usually finished my work within the first few minutes of class. In English, I would listen to stories the other male students would tell about Mrs. Landry. Mrs. Landry was the regular English teacher over the class I was now attending. She was on a short sabbatical for unknown reasons but was scheduled to return soon. She returned to work a couple of weeks after I got there, and I was able to see what all the fuss was about. She was, as most of the other guys has said, beautiful. She stood six feet tall with a slim, curvy figure, long brown hair, and big brown eyes. She was smart, well educated, and wealthy; I was instantly in love.

I immediately started flirting, and much to my surprise, she seemed to show some interest in me. This was especially dangerous for several reasons. One, she could lose her job, and two, she was married to a doctor. I won't go into all the details, but I'll tell you, what started out as simply flirting grew into a whole lot more. I graduated high school in this treatment facility, on schedule in late May, but I still needed at least a month before I could graduate the program. I was attending regular twelve-step meetings as part of the treatment requirements, though I never believed I was truly an alcoholic or drug addict. At this early point in my addiction, I thought all my problems stemmed from JJ "ratting" me out, not from my inability to maintain my drug usage.

I graduated in late June and returned home to my father's house to live. I professed to have had a spiritual awakening as a result of working the twelve steps, that I had seen the error of my ways and would travel that road no more. It was the year 1988, and the words *addiction* and *12-Step Program* were not as commonly heard or talked about as they are today. My family, as did many people, believed that addiction was an ailment which could be cured if caught in time. I graduated the program by complying with the rules and saying what everyone wanted to hear, though I didn't believe it applied to me. As soon as I got home, I went to court to make a plea bargain. Because this was my first felony, I received two years probation with various conditions. I had to perform 160 hours of community service, submit to random drug screens, and pay restitution to the school for the damages I had done. Most people would have considered the reality of probation and the consequences that followed a violation as a wakeup call. I, being so much smarter than everyone else, figured as long as I didn't smoke weed, I could party three weeks out of each month and still pass my drug tests.

Before I left the treatment facility, Dana, the teacher I had been flirting with, gave me a phone number and a time and date to call her. Dana was nine years older than me and had endured five long years of a miserable marriage. I was eighteen, fearless, full of passion, and able to tell her exactly what I knew she wanted to hear. I took a job waiting tables at a restaurant close to her home. We started seeing each other as often as she could get out of the house, with little or no regard for what her husband might be thinking.

Her husband eventually became suspicious, so he set us up. He told her he had a doctor's convention in Austin for the upcoming weekend. She called to make arrangements for me to stay the weekend with her. After working Friday night, I drove to her house, parked down the street, and slipped inside. We had a few drinks, I took a shower, and we got into her bed. It was a good thing she had closed and locked her bedroom door as a just-in-case precaution, because just as we started fooling around, we heard the front door open. Horrified, I jumped from the bed, grabbed my clothing from the floor, and headed for the window. "You can't get out that way," she said as I lifted the blinds. I knew she was right when I saw the burglar bars on the outside of the window, so I turned back tofind another option. I quickly realized there was no other option; there was noway out except through the bedroom door, which her husband now stood outside of, beating on it and demanding to be let in.

I could tell he was about to come through the door whether she opened it or not, so I made for the closet. I crawled behind a lot of clothing that hung to the floor, praying he would not find me. He seemed to know exactly where I was, because shortly after the bedroom door flung open, the closet light came on. He started searching through the clothes, found and grabbed my ankle, and pulled me from the closet. Much to my relief, he seemed more disgusted with her than angry with me. I was thankful he was a thirty-five-year-old doctor and not a twenty-five-year-old construction worker, or things might have gone a lot differently. I grabbed my clothes and quietly left, swearing that the relationship was over.

SEEING THE DEMON

I WAS LIVING AT MY FATHER'S HOUSE AND commuting about fifty miles to and from work. Because my nights were no longer occupied with Mrs. Landry, I started going out after work with some newfound friends. It didn't take long before I became buddies with a guy who snorted a lot of cocaine. One night after work, I followed him on a run to score some coke. We decided to split an eight ball, which would give me 1.75 grams of coke. I remained in my car while he ran into an apartment complex to retrieve the dope. A short while later, he reappeared with the ball already divided into two baggies. I chose the one I wanted and told him I'd see him later, that I had prior plans with the coke and my girlfriend. I had made no prior plans, but because I wanted to shoot the coke, not snort it, I could not hang with him. It's funny how people who snort cocaine think they don't have a problem. They call themselves "recreational users" and will quickly shy away from someone who shoots it or smokes it. I guess I felt the same way, because

I didn't want anyone to know I was one of those "needle-loving junkies."

It took me three attempts before finding a late-night pharmacy that would sell me the syringes I needed. I now had my coke, points, and a lot of stomach- churning desire. I just needed to get home to perform the act.

I got home about 11:30 p.m. on a weeknight, so my father had long since gone to bed. I grabbed a glass of warm water and a spoon and headed for my bedroom. I closed and locked the bedroom door behind me and turned off the overhead light. I opened the closet door and turned on the closet light so I could see to rig up the dope. I hadn't shot any coke in almost six months, so I wanted to make sure I did a big shot in order to really get off. Against my better judgment, I put about a half a gram of coke in the spoon, added the water, and mixed it up. I knew if the dope was good, then I would draw up more units in the syringe than the amount of water used. In other words, if I used 30 units of water, then I should draw back around 40 units of water/dope mixture. In this case, I drew back 60 units of water/dope mix. A voice in my head said, *It'll be all right,* as I stuck the needle in and delivered the massive shot.

As I pulled the needle from my arm, I was surprised by the much stronger ether taste I was having compared with what I remembered. Whenever a person shoots cocaine, there is a slight taste of something like medicinal ether that precedes the effects. Following the taste came the deafening *womp, womp, womp* sounds that accompany the enormous rush. For a split second, this rush seemed like the others from long ago, and then, alarmingly, it became different.

The rush escalated to the point I could not hold myself up. I was sitting on the side of my bed next to the open closet when I did the shot. As the rush intensified and the room began to violently shake, I slipped off the bed onto the floor. Large amounts of drool ran down my chin as I lay face down on the carpet, trying to regain my motor control. I reached up with my left hand and grabbed the closet door handle and placed my right arm on the bed. I was struggling to stop my body from the uncontrollable rocking motion I was currently undergoing. In an attempt to pull myself from the floor, I caught a glimpse of my reflection in the mirror on the door. I was watching and trying to stop myself from involuntarily shaking when I saw a reflection of something sitting on my bed, directly behind me.

Alarmed to now see something that had not been there before, I sobered up enough to stand and turn to see what it was. Sitting there in plain sight was a creature unlike anything I had ever seen outside of a horror movie.

The violent shaking stopped as I focused in on what resembled the form of a man blended with the form of a snake. I froze and blinked twice before deciding what I saw was really there. Sitting in the middle of my bed was a pale, yellowish-grey, hairless creature. It had a large pumpkin-shaped bald head, and its skin was like that of a severely burned person. Its long arms were stretched out as it reclined against the headboard of my bed, resting its arms on top of the pillows. The abnormally long fingers of its hands tapered to fine points at the ends. Instead of legs, its lower body formed into a snake-like tail that trailed off the end of the bed. It had small, black, beady eyes and a large black mouth with black teeth. It wasn't until it started laughing at me that I truly started to panic. "What-tha," I said as I took a few steps away from the bed. As I did this, it sat upright and stopped laughing. It was if *it* was as alarmed that *I* could see it as I was to be seeing it.

I guess the creature realized it was visible to me, because it quickly flew off the far side of the bed into the shadows. Remember that the only light in the room was coming from the closet, which I was standing in front of. The creature disappeared into the darkness on the other side of the bed. Much to my horror, the quietness of the room was broken with what sounded like the long fingernails pulling across the carpet from underneath my bed. I thought it was crawling under the bed, across to where I was standing, to grab me by the ankles. I quickly jumped on top of the bed and watched for it to crawl out from under the bed into the light.

I was standing in the center of the bed, facing the open closet door, when I saw—in the reflection of the mirror—it pop up behind me. I turned my head and saw its evil face before it sprung from the shadows. It brushed against my left ankle as it flew across the bed and disappeared into the closet. At that point, I lost it and started screaming as I jumped backward across my bedroom. I crashed into my chest-of-drawers before I crumbled onto the floor, thinking I had to regain my footing and prepare to fight for my life. I turned on the overhead light as I heard my father open his bedroom door and start beating on mine. Unable to catch my breath or regain my senses, I frantically searched the room for my demonic enemy. My father was desperately pounding on my door and pleading with me to open it. Unsure of what I'd say but longing for the comfort of a protective parent, I opened the door.

"What's wrong, Carl? What's wrong with you?" he asked as he tried to convince me to take a seat on the bed beside him. I told him I had taken some acid earlier in the evening and had suffered from a horrifying hallucination.

I wasn't sure if my father knew anything about cocaine or the way it affects a person. Cocaine is an instantaneous drug. It comes on quickly and goes away quickly. If he knew that, then he would know I had done the coke in the bedroom, which would be something he wouldn't forgive quickly. With acid, the hallucinating affects can last for six to eight hours. Also, I had never heard of hallucinations being associated with cocaine. As far as I knew, what I saw sitting on my bed was real. But, I had no idea how to explain what or how I saw it.

I spent the next hour or so talking with him and trying to convince him I knew I had made a mistake taking the acid, and would never do it again. During that hour, the effects of the coke wore off, and all I could think about was the need to do another shot. He went back to bed, and I went back to my room, where despite the frightening encounter I'd had, I spent the rest of the night shooting up the remainder of the cocaine.

———— ◆ ◆ ◆ ————

Nakot was panting heavily as he exited Carl's home. He stopped in the backyard and gazed back, wondering what had just happened.

Just as expected, Kansra arrived in a flash of light. "Nakot, why are you out here in the yard? I thought you told me you felt confident about tonight being the night for an overdose. What happened? And why do you look so alarmed?" Nakot continued to stare at the house and pant heavily. "Answer me!"

Kansra roared as fire and black smoke poured from his nostrils.

"I'm trying, sire," Nakot sheepishly responded. "If you'll give me a chance." Nakot lowered his gaze to the ground and started pacing back and forth in front of Kansra. "I don't understand what happened, sire. Everything was going along great. The boy had plenty of the drug they call cocaine at his disposal. I convinced him to do a shot that should have stopped his heart. The boy did the shot and started convulsing. He lost control of his bodily functions and fell off his bed. I'm sitting there on his bed laughing, waiting to escort his soul to you, when I'm overwhelmed by an excruciating white light. It was blinding, so I turned away from it. When I turned back, I saw Jasos and Ditri helping the boy up. I sat up in the bed and started to ask them what they were doing there, when they started rebuking me in the name of Christ. I had no choice but to flee as quickly as possible. Also, I truly think the boy saw me."

"What?" Kansra shouted, alarmed. "Why do you think the boy saw you?"

Nakot paused for a moment before he looked at Kansra. "Because,the very moment God's angels grabbed the boy and started helping him up, he looked directly at me and gasped. That's when Jasos started rebuking me in the name of Christ. I flew into the shadows and attempted to hide under the bed. The boy jumped on top of the bed as he was running from me. For fear he might really see me if I crawled out into the light, I tried to remain in the shadows. I don't know how he could see me, but I know he could. He was facing away from me when I came out from under the bed. I think he saw my reflection in a mirror, because he turned toward me—and screamed when he looked upon my face."

Now Kansra was pacing back and forth, staring at the ground. "Why would the boy have been able to see you?" he mumbled to himself as he paced. "And, why would God have sent both Ditri and Jasos to render him aid?"

Nakot stood there quietly shaking his head, as if to silently say, "I don't know."

"Come, Nakot," Kansra ordered. "Let's go back into the house to see what's going on." The two reappeared in the corner of the bedroom. Ditri and Jasos were both standing at the foot of Carl's bed, facing Kansra and Nakot, as if they were waiting for them to appear. Ditri and Jasos's magnificent presence was enough to make Nakot cower behind Kansra like a small child.

"Hello, Kansra," Jasos said in a calm, clear voice. "What brings you here?"

Kansra stared at Jasos for a moment before answering, "I'm here because one of my soldiers called upon me. He told me a boy that belongs to me was assisted by the two of you. He also told me the boy was able to see him. Now, I'd like to know why you two are here. And, was that boy really able to see my soldier?"

Jasos remained silent but never took his gaze off Kansra. Ditri calmly said,

"God sent us, to protect the boy's life."

"Why?" asked Kansra. "That boy hasn't asked for the gift of salvation; therefore, he is not a child of God. So why did God send the both of you to protect him? That kind of protection is supposed to be reserved for followers of Christ, not for lost drug addicts."

"God commanded, and we obeyed."

"Bahh," roared Kansra, "obey, obey, obey. Don't talk to me condescendingly about obeying."

Kansra grabbed Nakot by the wrist and left the bedroom. Kansra reappeared in the backyard, dragging Nakot along behind him as a toddler might drag a rag doll.

"Sire. Please, sire," cried Nakot as he struggled to gain his footing.

Kansra released him and moved a few feet away. "I don't know what God is up to with this boy, but this war is not over yet," Kansra said with an evil grown.

Nakot nervously looked up to Kansra. "Do you think God is going to call upon this boy to be one of Christ's disciples?"

Kansra turned away from Nakot and stared up at the moon as he started to speak. "Well, He might. The truth is, God calls upon many, but few listen to Him.

And, of that few, only a few take action." Kansra paused before he turned back to face Nakot. "Now, we've got a good hold on the boy through the drugs. I want you to recruit whatever help you need from the other soldiers and destroy the boy's life. You need to influence destruction in the lives of whomever he loves and whoever loves him. He's already tried one suicide, so spiral his life downward until he loses all hope and takes his own life.

Then we will get his soul—and possibly the should of those aroundhim."

"Yes, sire," responded Nakot with great enthusiasm as he returned to hell to recruit his help.

Kansra watched Nakot vanish as he sat there pondering the recent events.

"Great!" he mumbled to himself. "Don't tell me I've appointed Nakot to a challenge that may one day be called upon by God."

Kansra waited patiently for Satan's arrival. He knew the moment he saw Ditri and Jasos, his master was about to get directly involved.

"Kansra," roared Satan as he appeared. "I sensed a great disturbance. Tell me, what has taken place here."

"Kansra took a deep breath before explaining all that had taken place since he appointed Nakot to Carl.

"Humph," remarked Satan. "Ditri and Jasos? God must be up to something. What is your retaliatory plan?"

"Well, sire, I ordered Nakot back to hell to recruit assistance for the days to come. I told him to focus on both Carl and whomever he cares for. I believe if we can use his actions to separate him from all those who care for him, then we can convince him there's no hope. If he has no hope, then taking his own life will seem like the easy way out."

"Good!" exclaimed Satan in a cold, somber voice. "I do not know what God is up to, but it is up to you to stop it. I trust you know that if Nakot fails, you fail."

Before Kansra could look up at his master, Satan was gone.

CONSEQUENCES

DANA'S HUSBAND HAD MOVED OUT THE day after he discovered me in their closet. After a few weeks, her life seemed to calm down, and we started seeing each other again. Within a few short months, they were divorced, and I moved in with her. It wasn't long before the terrifying memories of that night at my father's house started dwindling away. The voice in my head started telling me, *Man, you just did way too much coke in one shot. That's the only reason you hallucinated so badly. As long as you don't put that much in the spoon, you can still do coke without tripping out.*

I finally listened to the voice and started disappearing without notice for twenty-four to forty-eight hours at a time. From time to time, I would get off work, have a few drinks with other co-workers, and in a buzzed state of mind, go and get an eight ball of coke. I would rent a room at a cheap motel, lock myself in with a pack of points and the dope, and go to town. Sure enough, I found that if I didn't put enough coke in a shot to borderline overdosing, the demons seemed to stay away.

I still suffered with terrible paranoia, but I didn't see any terrifying creatures sitting on the bed. The nights I would disappear were terrible for Dana, because she would be left alone wondering what had become of me and not knowing if she would see me alive again.

Though I professed to love her, and truly thought I did, at times, I was unable to overcome the strong obsession to get high. That obsession would cause me to disappear without so much as a phone call. The obsession I had for cocaine soon became a real problem or me. I found myself unable to refrain from using it long enough for my system to clean out before reporting for probation. It didn't take long before I figured out my probation officer wasn't my friend. After failing two drug screens in three months, he sentenced me to not more than one year of confinement in a state restitution center. He explained this was my last shot to get it right before they revoked my probation and sentenced me to do my two years in prison.

As I soon learned, the restitution center was something like a state-run facility. There was a probation officer, along with a few counselors, assigned to the facility five days a week. To graduate the program, one must complete a set of requirements for six different phases or spend one full year before being discharged. Part of the requirements was to obtain and keep full-time employment. Each inmate was required to relinquish their paycheck to the staff at the center. The staff put the money into an individual inmate account. A certain portion of the money would be drawn out each month to pay for probation fees, restitution dues, and the ten-dollar-a-day requirement to stay at the facility. We were taken to and from work in a large white van. The hours we were signed out from the center had to coincide with the amount of hours on our paychecks.

There were no bars on the facility, and we could go outside unsupervised to play basketball during the day as long as it wasn't raining. Though there was no one there who would force us to stay, if an inmate was kicked out or ran off, a felony warrant was immediately issued. It didn't take me long to find a job waiting tables at a restaurant that didn't mind my situation. The restaurant employed a few fellow inmates and didn't ask too many questions, which was cool, because I didn't want to provide too many answers. As with the staff of any restaurant, there were a few individuals who really liked to party with the help of pharmaceuticals, and I always seemed to buddy up with them. I started buying acid and ecstasy and taking it back into the center with me. Me and a buddy I made friends with in there would trip on the weekends when there was little staff to notice.

Several of the other inmates were in there for crimes related to their usage of something called crack. I had heard on the news of the horrors of this new drug because of its unprecedented ability to instantly transform someone into a full-blown crack addict. I had never seen crack or even talked to anyone who had seen crack, but my curiosity and lack of fear for trying something new got me started asking questions. A couple of guys told me the effects of a hit of crack greatly resembled a shot of coke and that I didn't have to worry about getting a hard-to-find syringe.

I decided I really wanted to try it, so I started keeping some of my tips each night. It took me a couple of nights to collect fifty dollars to give to a "friend" so he could score us some crack. He worked as a cook at a different restaurant on a tougher side of town. I, still being naïve enough to believe all drug dealers or drug addicts were honest, gave him my money with the full expectations of him returning from work the next day with my crack. As you might have guessed, instead of giving me the dope, he gave me some crazy story of how he got ripped off. It took several time of my losing my money before someone brought me back some crack. I hated being taken advantage of, but the overwhelming desire to get high caused me to keep trying. I smoked it and got high, but I failed to see what all the fuss was about. To me, the rush that accompanied the crack was nothing in comparison to the rush of a good shot. Because I wasn't thoroughly impressed and was tired of losing my money, I decided crack was not for me.

Due to my surroundings, I couldn't get as much as I wanted to, which is probably the only reason I successfully graduated the program. It took me nine months of "working" the twelve steps of a recovery program before I could successfully complete all six phases and graduate.

Somewhere in the midst of my stay, the strong obsession to get high seemed to dissipate. I decided that maybe my life had become unmanageable because I was shooting dope, so I would stop that and return to something less dangerous—like drinking.

THE GRIP OF HYDROCODONE

I LEFT THE FACILITY AND RETURNED home to live with Dana. I started drinking heavily every day, but my bouts with coke were few and far between. I made it through the next year with no other violations, so I was successfully discharged from my probation and free to do anything I wanted without fear of repercussions.

The treatment cent closed its doors abruptly, so Dana found herself without a job for the 1990-1991 school year. She and I got married in June of 1990 and, per her wishes, decided to move back to her hometown in northeast Louisiana. Nowhere, LA, is a small farming town in the delta of northern Louisiana. The town's population was just over a thousand people, with approximately eight hundred of them being cotton or soy bean farmers. I went through what you'd call a culture shock moving from the Houston area to this rural community. I knew nothing about farming but realized I had to learn the lingo in order to fit in. I started working for Dana's mother at their family-owned automotive parts store. Dana's father had passed away several years prior, and Dana had moved to Houston.

Dana's late father had bought her a large home in the center of town. Her mother's house was only a few blocks away, so she could regularly check on the house, and she paid a crew to maintain the yard. We moved into the big house, where at first it was kind of cool being the king of such a nice castle. After a couple of months, I really started missing the nightlife of the city and found myself with nothing to do but drink. Dana's mother, Sue, was a raging alcoholic, so at first, we got along great. Sue drank a fifth of Old Charter 8 year-old bourbon every single night. I had never been much of a whiskey drinker, but I soon learned how to be one.

Sue liked to cook but had no on at home to cook for. Dana and I probably spent five out of seven nights at her house, and she was probably at ours the other two. Sue was a very large woman. When I say "large," I don't mean tall. In fact, she only stood about 5'5", but she weighed just over three hundred pounds. She was an aggressive drunk who didn't mind telling someone what she thought about them. Her reputation preceded her throughout the town, and for the most part, people steered clear of her. In fact, I don't think anyone would have put up with her bitterness except she owned the only automotive and tractor parts store in town.

I worked for Sue during the day and drank whiskey with her at night. Dana was not much of a drinker because she had lost her father to alcoholism and knew she would lose her mother to it as well. I could tell she hated it when Sue and I got drunk and started arguing, but she was accustomed to the effects of heavy drinking. I think in some way it was almost normal for her. Once I got adjusted to the slower lifestyle of country living, I started having some fun. We took Dana's ski boat to a nearby lake almost every weekend, where we would rent a cabin and invite some friends. Dana's return home was a big buzz in the small town. At first we were very popular, and it seemed like we always had friends coming around.

Labor Day weekend, we rented a cabin at the lake and invited several friends along for the party. Once of the guys Dana invited, Chet, was an old schoolmate of hers. He was twenty-seven years old, flamboyantly gay, and living with his parents. Hardly anyone in town ever talked to Chet because he had just gotten out of jail and supposedly had AIDS. I had learned enough in the treatment hospital about AIDS to know that even if he did have it, he was no threat to us. He especially became cool in my book when, shortly after meeting him, he gave me a couple of pain pills. I had taken pain pills before, but only as prescribed. He gave me two Lorcet 10/650 pills, which would be equivalent to four of the pills I had taken before. In the past, when I had taken the prescribed amount, one

5-mg tablet every six hours, I had never experienced a Hydrocodone buzz. About forty-five minutes after I took the two 10-mg pills, I started feeling all warm and tingly, full of energy, and loose.
I got up on a slalom ski and seemed to ski better
and longer than ever before—I was spraying massive rooster tails and just about dragging my elbow
on the cuts. The pills made me feel stronger, and I
seemed to have more endurance. I was especially
proud of my skiing that day and enjoyed the praise
that was given to me by fellow skiers on the lake.
I decided that I didn't care what everyone else
thought of Chet, because he was about to become
my new best friend.

In the next few weeks, Chet started coming
over to the house more often. One afternoon, he
educated me on the various names and strengths
of pills and cough syrups. As a good student, I sat
there intently listening until I remembered I had
seen a large prescription bottle of cough syrup in
Sue's medicine cabinet.

Excited by the news, he agreed to ride over to
Sue's to see if it was "the good stuff." Relieved to
find no one at her house, I used a hidden key to
gain entry through the door. Once inside, I quickly
retrieved the bottle of syrup from the bathroom
and brought it to Chet for inspection. "Whoa, man,
this is it," he excitedly said.

I gazed down to see the label, which read,
Rutuss Green HC10mg/5ml. I had no idea what that

meant, but judging by Chet's reaction, I knew it must be good.

"Man, we need a cap off a bottle of NyQuil," he said. I'm sure he saw the puzzled look on my face because he explained, "Man, you don't want to do more than an ounce of this stuff, or you'll have the 'nods' so badly you won't be able to function."

"What are the nods?" I asked.

"Nodding off, man," he said as if I was stupid for asking.

I left for the bathroom thinking that I was never this precise with the amount of coke I was shooting; I couldn't imagine needing to be so precise with some cough syrup. Though I thought it was kind of ridiculous, I went and found a one-ounce measuring cap on top of a bottle of cold medicine. I returned with the cap, we each did a shot, and I put the bottle back where I found it. We left Sue's and returned to my house to chill and wait for the buzz to come on. I started thinking, *Man, the only bad thing about this stuff is you have to wait so long.*

With coke it's an instant high.

I was thinking about asking Chet if he could get some cocaine when the first wave of warm tingles started flushing through my body. I was surprised because it had only been about twenty minutes since we did the shots. Apparently he was getting off, too, because he said, "Yeah, man, this stuff's way better than pills. It gets you off faster and harder, and it seems to be a clearer buzz." I agreed with him; I was buzzing way better from that ounce of syrup that I had from those pills. I decided that day I had finally found what I was searching for with this brand new friend call Hydrocodone.

Dana was not around that afternoon, and Chet left before she got home. I decided I should use her to get more of that syrup. I couldn't steal the bottle without Sue eventually noticing it missing. She would have known Dana hadn't taken it, which would have left only me, and I didn't want that kind of attention. When Dana came walking through the door, she was greeted by the sounds of me in the bathroom, coughing up a lung. She appeared in the doorway and asked, "Carl, are you all right?"

I calmly replied, "I don't know, baby. I haven't said anything, but I haven't been feeling very well for the last couple of days, and now I've developed this stupid cough." As I getting the last of these words out, I broke off into a violent coughing spell and turned to lean over the open toilet.

I smiled a grin-less smile when I heard her say, "Ohh, baby, let me go to Mom's to see if I can find you some medicine."

Afraid she might not return with the right stuff, I told her I had already taken some Robitussen, but it had no effect on my terrible cough. As she was walking out the door, she assured me her mother had something that would knock my cough out. Instead of saying, anything, I broke into another round of violent coughing, which I kept up until I heard her get into her car. She was gone about thirty minutes before I saw her pull back up in the drive-way and once again, I greeted her with another bout of hard coughing as she walked through the door.

"Now be careful with this stuff," she said. "You don't need to take very much of it because it's really strong."

Because I was still buzzing heavily from the ounce I had taken earlier, I only took a teaspoon as directed, and put the bottle away. There was only an ounce or so left in the 16-ounce bottle, so Sue told Dana she would get me another bottle the next day. I learned that in this small-town life, where everybody knew everybody, a doctor's approval wasn't needed to refill the syrup. Dana's family had been lifelong friends with the owners of the three different pharmacies in town, and they didn't seem to have a problem refilling the prescription. I started bouncing from pharmacy to pharmacy, refilling the bottles as often as I could. My tolerance for the stuff grew pretty quickly, so it started taking two to three ounces of syrup to get me through the day. After a couple of months, the pharmacists decided I had had enough, so they cut me off. They each told me they could do nothing without a new prescription from the doctor, basically going back to doing things the way it was supposed to be done in the first place.

The result of being cut off sent me into my first round of withdrawal. I had never heard of withdrawal symptoms being associated with anything but heroin. At the time, I didn't know Hydrocodone was a synthetic opiate and that opium was what made heroin so addictive. I was unsure of what was wrong with me, but I somehow knew a shot of syrup would fix it. I called Chet to see if he could help. He said he could sell me some pain pills, but that the syrup was almost impossible to get. I bought all the pills he would spare and was relieved that they did the job of suppressing the overwhelming anxiousness, tiredness, and restlessness I was experiencing.

Dana and I decided to take a trip back to Texas to see my family and some of her friends. We stayed one of the nights with my mother before going on to Houston to see her friends. My mother was a nurse working at a small private practice in town, so I figured she might have some syrup or pills tucked away somewhere in her bedroom or bathroom. We arrived at her house, where we ate dinner and sat around telling her stories of our new home and all the splendors of quiet, country living.

While she and Dana were talking and cleaning the kitchen, I snuck into her room. I searched high and low throughout the bathroom and bedroom before I conceded to the fact there was nothing good to find. I was about to leave her bedroom when I noticed a couple of prescription pads, along with some written prescriptions, lying in a basket on top of her dresser. I grabbed one of the pads and one of the written scripts, stuck it in my pocket, and exited the room. I quickly walked outside to the car, where I hit them in the trunk. I had no idea of how to write a prescription, but I knew I could figure it out. We finished out the weekend and returned home to Nowhere, where I quickly called Chet to request another round of pills.

He came over the next day while I was home alone, and I told him I had come into possession of a script pad but wasn't sure how to use it. As it turned out, the reason Chet was living with his parents was because he had just gotten out of prison for forging prescriptions. He was excited to see the pad and even more excited that I was going to be the one using it. He told me he couldn't do it because he had been busted in Nowhere and that he was known in every pharmacy for fifty miles. He told me to get a piece of paper and start duplicating what he wrote and to make my handwriting resemble the writing of the already written script. I practiced on several sheets of paper before we agreed that my version of the doctor's writing, and especially his signature, was a very close match. He explained what the strange symbols meant and how to use them correctly in order to avoid suspicion. I went through several sheets of paper practicing my forgery skills before I attempted to write my first script for Rutuss Green.

I carried the script to one of the local pharmacists, as if I had not a care in the world. I felt safe because of the long-time friendship the pharmacist had with my wife's family. As I expected, they asked no questions while filling the prescription, which confirmed in my mind I had written it correctly. For the next few months, I made several rounds to the different pharmacies presenting fake scripts without caution, as if what I was doing was legal. One day, at a particular pharmacy, I learned that the pharmacist has the final say about filling a prescription. I caught a break that day; the pharmacist didn't call the doctor or the police—he simply refused to fill the script. He explained that if he felt the doctor was unjustly writing me scripts for narcotics, then he could refuse to fill them and even call the authorities on that doctor if necessary. I could tell by the way he was explaining all of that it was a warning I had better heed.

Apparently, all of the local pharmacists got together and decided to cut me off, because I was denied service at each pharmacy. I know now they were only trying to help me, but at the time, with terrible withdrawals coming on, I didn't think of them as friends. I went through withdrawal and got off Hydocodone without going to jail. I say it like that because that was the only time I could make that statement.

THE GRIP OF CRACK

AFTER A COUPLE OF WEEKS, I WAS BACK up on my feet and seemed to be functioning normally. This was my first real encounter with what I'll call the "happy days" syndrome. I discovered that after going through a withdrawal, there comes a phase where the body and mind feel great, hence the "happy days." I don't know if it's because my body was clean and clear of the drugs or that the low of the withdrawal had finally subsided. Either way, I remarkably felt full of energy and excited to be alive for about two weeks. After a couple of weeks of the happy days, the joy of being sober abruptly ended; I started drinking again, heaver than ever. I found that when I was on the Hydrocodone every day,I didn't need to drink as much. I also found out that because of my inability to get any more Hydrocodone, it seemed to take more alcohol to fill the void.

Dana and I went to a friend's house one night to grill some steaks and have some drinks. After a couple of drinks, her friend asked if we would like to join them in doing a line of coke. I was surprised but very happy to hear Dana say, "Sure, why not?" We spent the remainder of the evening drinking, snorting coke, and talking in circles about absolutely nothing. The evening ended, and we went home without an incident from me. I think that because we went home, and I didn't end up running off to look for more coke, Dana thought it was probably going to be safe to occasionally use it. The next weekend arrived, and we decided to get an eight ball of coke. We scored the coke from her friends and spent the weekend snorting lines here and there, as if I had become someone who could now "handle" it recreationally. These few weeks of flirting with cocaine were like the calm before the storm.

The following week seemed pretty normal, but that Friday was a life- changing day for me. Friday evening came, and we went to Sue's for dinner. Dana and I had several drinks before and after the meal and decided to try to get some more coke. We left Sue's and went home to call her friends. Her friend answered the phone but told her they weren't doing anything that weekend for whatever reason. By this time, we had both built up a pretty good buzz on alcohol, which manifested a strong desire to do find some coke. I decided I would head out to the bar on the outskirts of town to see if I could "get lucky."

There were two bars located just off the highway, about a mile from town.

It appeared that a soybean field and a bayou were all that separated the two establishments until you walked inside the bars. The first one I came to was occupied by all white people. I walked in, ordered a beer, and took a seat at the end of the bar. I shamelessly approached a couple of likely candidates but was quickly turned away. On my third attempt, the guy told me he didn't have any, but I might have better luck across the bayou. I knew the bar across the bayou was bigger and always seemed to have a larger crowd; my only concern was that my white presence might not be welcome in that all-black crowd. When it came to getting high, self-preservation often took a backseat ride.

Nervous but hopeful, I left the all-white bar and headed across the bayou. I pulled off the highway and stopped the car on the edge of the parking lot. I rolled down the passenger window and started whistling to a few different individuals. Two of the guys I whistled at looked at me as if I was crazy before they turned and walked away. I was starting to think I was wasting my time and should probably leave while I still could when this one guy stepped up to my window and said, "Say, man, whatcha looking for?"

"An eight ball," I quickly replied.

He looked at me kind of funny and said, "Man, how much money you trying to spend?"

Thinking that, given the circumstances, I might have to pay a little more than the usual $125, I said, "Oh, I don't know, say one twenty-five to one fifty."

I was a little taken back when the guy started laughing at me and said, "Hold on, man, I'll go get your stuff, but don't talk to nobody else out here, 'cause they be trying to get ya."

The stranger walked away, and I sat there wondering what he meant when he said, "They be trying to get ya." I played football with several black guys in high school, and a couple of them, I called friends. We were friends at school and in the locker room, but that was about it. I never visited them at their home or even rode through their neighborhoods, much less drove up to where they were drinking and decided to hang out. I started freaking out, thinking the car door was going to fly open at any minute, and I would be jerked from the car and beat senseless. My instincts for self preservation took over, and I decided to get out of there. I cranked my car and started to pull away when I saw in the rear view mirror the stranger running after me, waving his arms.

I stopped the car and slightly rolled down the passenger window. He told me to let him in to make the deal, so I unlocked the door. He sat down in the passenger seat and pulled up a baggie filled with what looked like little rocks. I turned on the overhead light and saw that he had brought me $150 worth of crack.

"Ohh, man, I wanted an eight ball of powder. I don't smoke crack."

In aggravation, he looked at me and said, "Say, man, there ain't no powder out here nowhere. Now you didn't say you was lookin' for powder, and he ain't gonna take this back, so you mize-well smoke it. Besides, man, this is some good stuff; you gonna like this stuff."

I didn't believe what he was saying about the fact there was no powder,but I knew I couldn't contest it. I figured this was all I was going to get, so I quickly geared my mind around smoking crack. Both times I had smoked crack was when I lived at the restitution center. The first time I smoke it, we used a Coke can and some ashes for a smoking apparatus; the second time, we used a pipe made from an antenna stuffed with a small piece of copper scouring pad. I had learned enough from those two times to know I could make a pipe of some sort out of materials lying around the house. I drove home devising in my mind how I was going to construct a pipe and convince Dana to try it. I walked in the door with a disappointed look on my face and said, "Well, you're not going to believe this."

She looked at me with a look like, "I told you so" and said, "What happened? You got ripped off, didn't you?"

"Well, not exactly," I said as I turned toward the cellar door, "but we're going to have to smoke it."

"Smoke it? What do you mean, 'smoke it?"

I had already started walking down the cellar stairs to look for an antenna attached to an old radio when I replied. "Well, this coke has already been rocked up for free-basing." I knew if I said I had a bag of crack, Dana would have a fit. I still don't know the difference between free-basing cocaine and smoking crack, but I knew it would sound better for her to hear free-basing. I reached the bottom o the stairs and turned toward a pile of old junk that had accumulated in a corner of the basement. I guess Dana was processing what I said, because she didn't ask any more questions while I was down there. I found an old radio, grabbed a screw driver, and removed the antenna. I used a hacksaw to cut a five- inch section from the base of the antenna and started back up the stairs.

At the top of the stairs, I turned to walk through the kitchen to the sink area. Under the sink, I found the box of Chore Boy brand scouring pads I had noticed while putting cleaning supplies away. I grabbed some scissors and cut a small piece of the Chore Boy, rolled it up, and packed it into the end of the cut section of antenna. I knew Dana was curious, but she asked no questions while she observed my actions. I walked from the kitchen to the bedroom, where I removed a wire clothes hanger from the closet. I straightened out the hook to use as a push for the pipe. I had seen all this done at the restitution center, so I was able to perform these tasks as if I knew exactly what I was doing. I packed the scouring pad into the end of the pipe with the push wire and loaded a large rock on top of it. I grabbed a cigarette lighter, lit it, and sucked the flame across the rock and into the pipe. The rock started sizzling, crackling, and melting right before my eyes. My lungs filled with smoke to the point

I could hold no more, I held it in for as long as I could before I exhaled.

The moment the smoke started leaving my mouth, the familiar sound of *womp, womp, womp* filled my ears. The room began to shake, and I had to grab hold of the dresser to stabilize myself. Apparently the two times I had tried crack before, I had done too small a piece, the dope wasn't very good, or I improperly smoked it. Either way, this time, I was rushing just like I had done a large shot of cocaine. After several minutes, I regained my senses enough to form a smile at the fact I had a newfound friend called crack cocaine.

I cooled the pipe down a little bit then loaded a large piece on it for Dana. I instructed her on the proper techniques in order to get a good hit, lit the lighter, and told her to start sucking in the flame. I watched the rock melt away and her eyes grow really large as she waved her hand for me to pull the flame away. I told her to hold it as long as she could before expelling the smoke. As she exhaled, her jaw dropped and her eyes grew wide. I knew she was rushing; she wouldn't answer me when I asked if she was all right. After a couple of minutes, she agreed with me that this was a whole lot better high than just snorting coke.

We stayed up all night, smoking rock after rock until we ran out the next day. This is when we realized the major difference between smoking crack and snorting coke: the come down. Coming down from snorting coke is unpleasant but manageable. As soon as I started coming down from the last hit, I wanted more. *Man, I just need one more good blast,* was all I could think about. Dana must have been feeling the same way, because she didn't protest when I told her I was going to make another run to the bar.

I drove to the ATM, withdrew $200, and headed for the bar. This little routine went on for the next week. We each called in sick to our work, locked ourselves in the house, and just smoked crack. The only time I would leave the house was to make runs to the bar to re-up the supply. Dana would fall asleep after a twenty-four to thirty-six-hour run, but I did not. I stayed up smoking crack for five full days. On that last day, I started hallucinating. I saw all kinds of shadows moving, heard strange noises, and thought people were sneaking around inside the house. I probably would have freaked out, but Dana was there to tell me I was hallucinating. She finally convinced me to lay it down and get some much-needed sleep, so I took a couple of 1-milligram Xanax pills and sat down in my recliner.

I don't remember falling to sleep. I only remember waking up to some unfamiliar surroundings. I remember thinking, *Man, this is not my recliner or even my bed. Dude, this is a hospital bed.* I sat up and looked around, trying desperately to remember something that would explain how I had gotten there.

A nurse walked through the door. "Oh, I see you're finally waking up," she said. "Let me go and get your wife." She left the room, and I sat there wondering how I could have ended up in there without a single memory of the trip.

Dana walked in and filled me in on the chain of events that had taken place over the last two days. She told me that when I fell asleep in the chair, I would occasionally jerk violently and almost fall out onto the floor. She said she tried to wake me so I would move to the bed, but I wouldn't wake up. After a full twenty- four hours of trying to wake me, she freaked out and called her mother. They both became alarmed because I would not respond to their attempts to revive me, so they called 911. Apparently, an ambulance came to the house; paramedics loaded me up and took me to a hospital some forty miles away. Dana told them I had used a lot of coke and taken a couple of Xanax to comedown.

Somehow, between all of them, they decided the best place for me was a hospital that had a wing designated for chemical dependency. I guess you could say I was completely out of it, because I was totally unaware that any of these events had transpired. Everyone was relieved when I woke up, but they were concerned about me because of the reasons I was there. I checked myself out of the hospital AMA (Against Medical Advice) and returned to Nowhere. No one suspected Dana of using the coke with me, so when she seemed to support my decision, everyone else simply backed off.

I didn't go back to work after that eventful week; in fact, my life was about to change drastically. We got back home, and the first thing I did was go and get some more crack. Dana didn't like the fact she had to go to work every day while I stayed home getting high, so she took a sabbatical from her teaching job. She told everyone it was so she could "help" me refrain from running off during the day while I was at home alone. It wasn't long before the drug dealers were stopping by the house and even accepting personal checks.

We had this one guy named Scotty who was a smoker but thought of himself as a dealer. His uncle would come into town every couple of weeks with large amounts of powder cocaine. Scotty would get an ounce on a front, meaning he didn't have to pay for it until he sold it, and bring it over to my house to cook it up. This routine went on for a couple of months before Scotty, being the smoke that he was, started messing up the money. His uncle gave him less coke to work with, which meant he came over spreading the wealth less often. Dana and I smoked crack day in and day out. We wrote checks for the dope with little or no regard for how much and how fast we were depleting the checking account. I dropped weight, and my clothes would no longer fit me, but I rarely left the house, so I didn't care.

In a few short months, we went through all the money in her checking and savings accounts, just over $27,000, and I had shed sixty-five pounds of weight. Now, because I wasn't a heavy person to begin with, I looked like death walking.

My mother saw me for a brief moment during this time and cried. By just one look, she knew I was into something much worse than anything before. I'll never forget that encounter; I was smiling as if nothing was wrong, and she, without remark, buried her face in her hands and cried. This took place on a one-week trip to Texas where everyone, including me, thought I needed some time away from Nowhere.

After a full week of eating, drinking, and sleeping, I felt rejuvenated and ready to get back to the dope. The only problem was, we no longer had a flowing source of capital, so getting high became somewhat of a challenge, I wrote bad checks, stole anything of value, and even sold off my clothes in order to get a few rocks. I broke into Sue's store one night and stole all her petty cash fund. She, along with everyone else, knew that I did it, but no one could prove it. I was no longer welcome in the town because everyone knew I was strung out on crack. I believe some people probably suspected Dana was using it, too; but for the most part, everyone felt sorry for her because she was just a victim, and I was just a scoundrel.

My grandmother called from San Antonio to invite Dana and me out to stay with her. She, as well as we, thought a geographical change might do the trick.

Dana and I packed enough clothing to stay for a while and headed west. To say the least, the geographical change didn't work; in fact, things only got worse. We were there only a few days before I figured out where the housing projects were in downtown. I started sneaking out as often as I could get money and catching a metro bus to downtown. Twice I took a taxi, but neither would take me into the projects for fear of being robbed. Though everyone seemed to make a big deal about how dangerous the place was, I never had any trouble finding and leaving with what I was looking for.

One night, Dana and I told my grandmother we wanted to go to dinner and a movie. I guess because Dana was going with me, my grandmother felt safe to loan us her Cadillac and give us some money. Dana and I got dressed and headed out about 5:00 that evening. We drove to a hardware store to buy the necessary parts to construct a pipe. For safety reasons, I told Dana to wait at the store while I drove to the projects to get the dope. The spot was only a couple of miles away, so I told her I would be back within twenty minutes.

As soon as I pulled into the area, I noticed a group of guys hanging on a corner beside an old, rusted playground area. Crack dealers are looking for a potential "lick" (a dope fiend) or a cop, so they thoroughly scope out every car. I slowed the car as I was passing in front of them and gave the universal nod for *What's up?*

As expected, one of the guys bounced up from a ledge he was leaning on and headed my way. I rolled down my window in time to hear him say, "What's up, man? What-cha lookin' for?"

"Fifty," I replied. We made the exchange, and he walked away. I had to pull down to the next driveway to turn the car around because the side street I was on was a dead end. I was pulling back up to the stop sign when I noticed the guys quickly abandoning their corner. When I got to the stop sign, I looked to my left and realized why they'd fled. A police car had turned into the neighborhood and was coming toward me. I went ahead and made the left turn toward the approaching cop, thinking that it might be less obvious if I turned toward him instead of away from him. Apparently, a young white guy driving a brand new Cadillac in one of the roughest housing projects in San Antonio was a little more than his curious nature could pass up. I passed the cop, got to the next stop sign, and turned right onto the main street heading back out of the downtown area.

I drove about a block before I saw them pull out onto the street behind me, turn on their lights, and quickly catch up. Unsure of what to do but knowing I had to pull over, I threw the dope under the floor mat and pulled off the main road.

There were two police officers in the car. With their hands on their pistols, they told me to exit the vehicle slowly with my hands where they could see them. As soon as I was out of the car, one of the officers told me to walk to the back of the car, turn around, and place my hands behind my back. While the one officer was placing me in handcuffs, the other one started searching through my grandmother's car. It wasn't long before the other cop exited the car with my crack and I was being read my rights. I was arrested for possession of a controlled substance and carted off to the county jail.

I was there about twelve hours before my grandmother and Dana were able to bail me out. The next day, we went to visit an attorney. For $3,500, he gladly took the case. He told us he didn't think it would be a problem because the police didn't follow the correct procedure in searching the car, so the evidence would be suppressed. It turned out he was right. The charges were dropped, and I never had to see the inside of a courtroom.

I, along with everyone else, realized the geographical location was not working, so Dana and I decided to head back to Louisiana. We returned to Nowhere, and I was forced to try to come down off this five-month crack run. I was miserable with and without the dope. I desperately wanted to get off of it, but the rush from hitting a large rock was all I could think about. In fact, when I started thinking about it, my stomach would start rolling and I often felt as if I needed to go to the bathroom. I had no way to come up with any money, and the obsession to get high consumed me.

One day, while Sue was gone, I drove over to her house to see if I could find something of value to trade for crack. I was pilfering through her bedroom when I heard her pull into the driveway. She must have known what I was up to, because she parked her car behind mine so I couldn't get out. I was coming out of her bedroom when she stormed through the back door carrying an aluminum baseball bat. I could tell by the look in her eyes she wasn't looking for an explanation—she wanted blood. "You no-good s-o-b, you came into my house to steal from me," she exclaimed as she raised the bat and charged toward me.

Realizing diplomacy was not going to work, I took off through the front door and ran around the house to where my car was parked. When I rounded the house, I saw she had blocked me in. By this time, she had come through the back door and started chasing me back past the front of the house and across her large lawn. She was screaming at me and telling me to go home to Texas, all while chasing after me and swinging her bat.

She was sixty-five years old and weighted over three hundred pounds.

Keeping myself clear from her swing radius wasn't very difficult physically, but I quickly lost patience with the humiliation of running from her like a scared dog. She quickly realized she wasn't going to catch me, so she turned back to get her car. I was almost to the end of her yard when she came driving out onto the grass after me. She didn't appear to be slowing down any, so I turned back toward the cover of some trees that sat beside her house. I reached a large tree with low- lying limbs and jumped up to grab hold of a branch.

Sue was drunk, as usual, while doing all of this, so I don't know if she was truly trying to kill me or if, in her drunken state, she missed the brake. All I know is I barely got my legs up and wrapped around the branch before she crashed into the tree beneath me. She wasn't going very fast, but it would have crushed my legs if I hadn't gotten out of her way.

"That's it! Play time's over!" I said as I climbed up a little higher and jumped over onto her roof. I ran over the rooftop to the back of the house, dropped off the roof, and ran to my car. In this small town, where auto theft was nonexistent, I had become accustomed to leaving my keys in the car. Sue must have known this, because she had removed my keys and locked the doors before she ever came inside.

By this time Sue was pulling around the house and heading straight for me.

I abandoned my car and headed for the one place I knew she couldn't follow—inside her house. She parked the car and jumped out with her bat in her hand. I ran inside and stopped in the middle of her spacious living room. Enough was enough. I was through running. I turned and waited for her to walk in. As expected, she came charging through the door with her bat raised, screaming, "You s-o-b, get out of my house."

Despite my earlier resolve, I backpedaled saying, "Sue, put the bat down and give me my keys. I'll gladly leave your house, but not without my car."

Sue had decided that because the car was in Dana's name, she was going to keep it; I was supposed to walk back to Texas. When she made that statement, I lost all patience with her, stopped retreating, and said, "Sue, put the bat down and give me my keys."

She swung the bat from side to side and walked toward me, screaming,

"Get out, get out, you s-o-b! Get out!"

Realizing she wasn't going to quit and the only way to retrieve my keys was to take them, I held my ground and said, "Sue, if you hit me with that bat, I'm going to hurt you."

She paused for a second, looked me in the eyes, and then swung away. I turned away from the swing, but the bat hit me hard on the back of my left shoulder. Without hesitation, I clinched up my right fist and swung it hard back around to the left side of her head. With a lot of force, my fist slammed into her left temple. She briefly yelped before she dropped the bat and crumbled to the floor.

"Ohh, no," I cried, thinking I might have killed her. After a few seconds, she began moaning. Realizing I had not killed her, I knelt down and searched through her pockets for my keys. I found them, left her lying there, and walked into the kitchen. I retrieved a large carving knife from a drawer and grabbed a full 32- ounce bottle of Gatorade from the fridge.

In the year 1990, a 32-ounce bottle of Gatorade was made of glass. I decided I was going to get some crack one way or the other, even if I had no money. I placed the knife under my seat and the Gatorade bottle between my legs. I drove out to the bar, pulled into the parking lot, and motioned for Jimmy to come get into the car.

Jimmy was one of the dealers who regularly came over to my house to sell me crack. I had done thousands of dollars in business with him, so I figured he was going to give me some crack whether he wanted to or not. Jimmy got into the car, and I pulled out of the parking lot. Instead of turning onto the dirt road that circled behind the bar, I started speeding down the highway. I think he realized something wasn't right, because he looked over at me and said, "Say, man, where you going? Just turn around and head back to the bar. I don't even know why you left. C'mon, man, let's go back to the bar."

Acting like nothing was wrong, I said, "It's cool, man. I'll turn around right up here. You got a good twenty-piece?"

He pulled out a Skoal can and removed the lid. "Yeah, man, I got the good stuff."

When the top came off I saw that the entire can was full of rocks. Without hesitation, I grabbed the full bottle of Gatorade with my right hand and swung it hard toward his face. Before Jimmy could even blink, the bottle connected with his forehead and exploded on impact. Nothing worked out like I thought it would. I expected Jimmy to be unconscious and the Gatorade bottle to stay intact.

Instead, I now had thirty-two ounces of orange-flavored Gatorade all over the inside of my car and a very stunned—but angry—Jimmy sitting in the passenger seat.

"Ooh, man, you didn't have to hit me," he said as he started picking up the pieces of crack that fell on the floorboard when he dropped the Skoal can. I pulled off the highway and snatched up all the rocks I could find. It was a race between him and me to grab the pieces. I didn't want to hit him with anything else, and I certainly didn't want to stab him, but I was going to get what I came for.

He apparently didn't want to mess with this crazy white boy, so he didn't say anything about the pieces I gathered. When all the pieces were up, he just asked me to take him back to the bar. I gave him a towel to wipe the blood from his forehead as we started the short drive back. We drove for about a minute in total silence before he said, "Man, Carl, I'da given ya some dope."

"Sorry, man," is all I said as I stopped the car on the highway in front of the bar so he could jump out. I rushed home so I could get high. I walked in the house, grabbed my pipe from a drawer, and melted down a twenty. I felt excitement and relief as the smoke filled my lungs. When I could hold no more, I placed the pipe in a towel and put the towel back in the drawer. I blew the smoke out and grabbed hold of the dresser for support. It was a big twenty, so I knew the rush was going to be heavy. Sure enough, my ears filled with that familiar *womp, womp* sound, and the room shook from side to side.

Just when I was reaching the peak of the rush, I heard a loud knock at the door. I walked across the bedroom to peer out the window, "Ohh, no," I said when I saw a patrol car sitting in my driveway and another one parked in the street.

I tried to regain my senses as I slowly walked toward the door. I paused in the middle of the living room, thinking if I didn't answer, maybe they would go away. Maybe they didn't know I was there. They knocked again, even louder this time, and followed it with, "Sir, we know you're in there. We need you to open the door, or we will."

I stepped into the bathroom to throw some water on my face, dried it off, and stepped to the door. I opened it as if nothing was wrong and acted as if I had no idea why they could possibly be there. They asked me to step outside, where they placed me in handcuffs and told me of the charges. They said I was under a twenty-four-hour safety hold. They had received a call from Sue telling them I could probably be of danger to myself or others and they should get me off the streets until I was in a better state of mind. I was angry, but I knew I had caught a break, because Sue didn't press charges for breaking and entering or assault.

I spent the night in the tiny city jail and got out the next afternoon. There was no one there to greet me, so I decided to walk home. My house was only a few blocks from the police station, so the walk wouldn't take that long. When I walked out and not even Dana was there to greet me, I realized I had hit bottom. I had managed to alienate myself from everyone, and I felt as if no one wanted me around. I had no job, no money, and no self-respect—all thanks to crack cocaine.

As bad as my life seemed at that moment all I could think about was hurrying home to smoke the other couple of rocks I had hidden. I arrived at my house, walked inside, and went straight to my dresser. I opened the drawer and knew Dana had found my stash because the dope and my pipe were gone. "That's it," I said to myself. "I don't want to do this anymore."

Tears welled in my eyes as I walked to the kitchen to pour myself a tall glass of bourbon and Coke. I made a strong drink, sat down at the table, and cried. I cried out loud for a couple of minutes before I regained my composure and gulped down my drink. I finished and made myself another one; after that, I made myself another one. The drunker I got, the grimmer my life appeared to me. I couldn't see a way up out of the hole I was in, but I knew I wanted out of it. That's when Dana walked through the door, and with her came the solution to all of my problems. Dana took medications for manic depression on a regular basis.

Besides the Prozac, which would do me no good, she kept scripts of 1-mg Xanax, 10-mgValium, and Halcion (sleeping pill).

I heard her walk into the bedroom and set her purse down in her usual spot, beside the dresser. She walked into the kitchen but had nothing to say as she leaned up against the kitchen sink. I guess the sight of me sitting there staring at the floor with tears flowing down my face took her by surprise. Without looking up, I asked, "How's Sue?"

Dana curtly replied, "She's okay, but she's afraid of you now. I mean, what's wrong with you? She's sixty-five years old. I don't even know what to say to you. She's my mother, and you hit her like a madman."

I sprang from my chair. "I'm the madman?" That crazy lady used her car to chase me all over her front yard. I had to climb a tree, jump onto the roof of her house, run over the top of the house, and drop down onto the back porch. She was trying to run over me, Dana. I had to go inside to end the chase. Then she followed me inside, swinging a baseball bat. I told her if she hit me with the bat, I was going to hurt her. Well, she hit me with the bat, and I hit her back."

Dana started to cry, so I stopped screaming at her. She was caught in the middle between her husband and her mother. She sat down on the floor, cryin' out loud, saying, "I don't know what to do, I don't know what to do. I can't believe this is my life. Why, why, oh my God, why?"

The anger left me, and the hopeless depression set back in. I was crying again and decided I was getting off of this ride. I turned and walked out of the kitchen, saying, "I'm sorry, Dana, I'm so sorry."

I walked to the bedroom, located her purse, and grabbed the bottles of pills. I quickly, but quietly, twisted off the top to each bottle and poured the contents into my hand. I didn't take the time to count, but I estimated the bounty to be around fifty pills. Without hesitation, I grabbed a half-empty glass of old water from the nightstand and started washing down the pills. It took about three gulps of water to successfully swallow all the meds. When I finished taking the drugs, I walked into the bathroom to take a shower. I didn't want to die unclean. Once I was in the shower, the gravity of the situation hit me. I realized I was only twenty years old, and I was about to die.

The thought of not seeing the next day caused my knees to get weak. I took a seat on the floor of the tub and cried. I guess the loud crying caught Dana's attention because she tried to open the locked bathroom door. She must have realized I was up to something, because she went to check her purse. She returned shortly and pounded on the door, saying in a frantic voice, "Carl, what have you done? Please let me in, baby, please."

The longer I sat there, the more frightened I got. I knew I didn't want to be found in the shower naked, so I got out to get dressed. When I opened the door, I found Dana sitting on the floor crying. I didn't know what to say or how to comfort her, so I stepped over her and walked into the bedroom. I got dressed and took a seat on the side of the bed. I contemplated the finality of death and realized I wasn't ready for it. I could feel the effects of the pills coming on, and I began to panic. I thought the only way to survive the pills was to stay awake, and the only way I was going to stay awake was if I had some crack. On a hunch, I grabbed Dana's wallet to search for money. Much to my surprise, I found sixty dollars inside. I grabbed the cash, dropped the wallet, and headed for the front door.

I realized I didn't have my keys, so I turned back to search for them. Dana must have known what I was doing, because she hid them and said, "Carl, you're not going anywhere. We've got to get you some help."

The pills really started to take effect, and my rationalization went out the window.

"There's no time," I said. "If I pass out, I'm going to die." As I was saying this, I believed it might be true.

I realized she wasn't going to give me my keys, so I decided to walk to the bar. Before I made it to the door she ran in front of me to try to prevent me from leaving. I convinced myself that my desire to smoke some crack had now become a life-or-death situation, and no one was going to stop me. I threw Dana out of my way and bolted the door. I took off running through people's yards and across empty lots, covertly dodging in and out of shadows for fear of being detected.

The effects of the pills finally took over, and I blacked out. The last thing I remember was crawling through a cemetery and seeing Dana's car passing by on a distant street. When I came out of the black out, I was in a cell at the city jail, trying to unlock the cell door with a plastic comb.

To this day, I don't know all the details about how I got there; I only know it was the next evening. I have no idea what took place in those twenty-four hours, and I suspect I never will. I was placed on a seventy-two-hour hold for fear that I was a danger to myself. I was placed in a cell by myself in the back of the jail.

Because I had not committed any offenses toward anyone else, I was more or less just being detained, not under arrest. The chief of police agreed to house me while Dana attempted to locate a treatment facility she could afford. Dana was allowed to visit and bring me food and snacks.

So there I was, feeling especially low because I was a junkie who was unsuccessful in my suicide attempt. It seemed that dying would be so much easier than facing the problems I had created for myself. I was very disappointed when I came to, so I tried to figure out a way to finish the job. Inside of a grocery sack filled with various snacks from Dana, I found a can of mixed nuts. I grabbed the can and removed the plastic lid, searching for the sharp, metal sealant lid underneath. Apparently, either the jailer or Dana realized it would not be smart to supply me with a sharp object, so they removed it. Disappointed to see it was not there but determined to finish the job, I decided to improvise.

I poured the contents of the can into the grocery bag. I then placed the can on its side and stomped down on it. I picked the can up, reopened it, and then crushed it again. I did this several times to weaken the crease in the tin in order to tear the can apart. I finally achieved what I was trying to do and tore the can into two parts. The result was what I was hoping for—a very sharp piece of steel. "Forgive me, Lord," is all I said as I cut open my left wrist.

I made several slices, searching for my artery. After minutes of cutting, I decided the paint was too much to continue. I had made three large incisions to my left wrist and two cuts between my shoulder and my elbow on the inside of my arm. Despite being in the right area, I was unable to locate and sever my artery. I was bleeding steadily from the wounds and might have eventually bled to death, but the jailer came around for a count. I didn't see him until I heard him say, "What-tha? What have you done?"

I didn't reply; I just watched him rush off to call for help. Shortly after, the paramedics showed up and carted me off to the local hospital. I'll never forget the way the nurses and doctors looked at me while they stitched up the cuts on my arm. I was taken back to the jail and placed in a padded room with nothing but my thoughts to keep me company. Sitting there in that padded cell, naked and cold, I thought to myself, *Man you are such a loser. You can't even kill yourself right.*

———◆●◆———

Nakot stood alone and miserable outside the jail waiting for Kansra to arrive.

"Well, Nakot," Kansra said as he suddenly became visible, "you're making a routine out of failing with this soul."

"It's not my fault, sire!" Nakot yelled with a pleading voice. "Jasos and Ditri have been with this boy the entire time. They were with him that night at the clinic. That's why I couldn't influence him into the pharmacy. Ditri said, 'You will fail at this attempt, as well, Nakot.'

"For months now, I have been successful in following your command. I have worked closely with several other soldiers, and together, our influence has caused the boy's life, as well as the lives of those around him, to spiral downward. I convinced him there was no hope and death would be an easy way out. The boy seemed to respond well to my influence and took more than enough pills to end his life. All seemed well, and then Jasos and Ditri showed up.

"Ditri rebuked me in the name of Christ, so again, I had to flee. Several times that night, I tried to return but was rebuked each time. When I was finally able to get back to the boy, he was sitting in a jail cell coming down off the pills. I immediately sat down beside him and resumed my influence toward suicide. He responded well. He tore a tin can apart and started slicing his wrist open. Then, as I was trying to tell him how to cut the main artery, Jasos showed up. Jasos got between me and the boy, so I couldn't clearly see what was going on. Sire, I believe Ditri sat down with the boy and placed a protective finger over his artery.

"Now, I know you're angry, but how am I supposed to claim this soul when it's so well protected?"

Kansra turned away from Nakot and stared at the outer walls of the jail for a while as he took in what Nakot told him. "Let's go, Nakot," demanded Kansra. "I want some answers."

Before the two could move, Satan appeared before them and angrily declared, "That's it! I've had enough! I will not lose this boy to God despite the protection from His 'holier-than-thou' angels. With that being said, Kansra, I am relieving you of your command. You are to return to a tempter status and assist Dakkas with anything he needs."

"Sire?" pleaded Kansra. "I can do—"

"Nothing!" Satan yelled. "You can do nothing except what I'm telling you to do. Now be gone from here."

Kansra instantly fled from sight. Satan turned his hideous face back toward the now trembling Nakot. "While I think you are unworthy to assist me, I will allow you to remain the boy's tempter.

Instead of Kansra, it will be me watching your progression. But, unlike Kansra, I do not listen to excuses or tolerate incompetence. Do I make myself clear?"

"Yes, sire. Perfectly!" Nakot assuredly replied.

Satan snarled. "Come with me. You are to observe, but remain silent."

Satan and Nakot appeared in the corner of the padded cell. Satan looked down at Carl and laughed before he turned his gaze toward Jasos and said, "Look at that pathetic piece of a human lying on the floor. He'll never amount to anything; you know that. Come now, that boy belongs to me. So why don't you two go and protect someone worthy of your protection."

"We are," replied Jasos. "Every one of these humans is worthy of our protection. God wants the entire race to become His children through the salvation of His Son, Jesus."

"Yes, I know," Satan barked, "but not if I can help it."

Ditri shook his head slowly from side to side.

Satan roared. "I have billions of followers who think they're following God. They pray several times a day and follow the teaching of one of my prophets. I've convinced them Jesus did not rise from the dead and their religion is the only true religion. I'm already winning this war on a global scale. Now, why don't you two go away and let me claim my prize? I mean, what can this one pitiful person ever do?"

Jasos maintained his strong stance in the face of Stan's malevolent glare. "We know that one day this boy will be a great messenger for Christ."

"That piece of trash?" Satan said as he started to chuckle. "Have you been watching his life?"

"Of course we have," Jasos said. "Lucifer, you are not the only one in pursuit of this soul."

Satan stood there speechless for a moment before he turned to Nakot. "Let's go. We'll catch this boy later." They returned to the parking lot of the jail to discuss a new strategy. "All right, Nakot," Satan firmly said, "It appears we are going to have a real fight on our hands."

With a sense of worry, Nakot looked up at Satan and said, "What did they mean when they said that boy's going to be 'a great messenger for Christ'?"

"Bahh!" roared Satan. "The most important thing I've learned over the centuries is, it's not over till it's over. Just because god has hopes for that boy doesn't mean the boy will materialize into anything that will be of a threat to us.

Now, the boy will probably go to one of those self-help treatment hospitals. Those programs will talk of finding a 'higher power.' Convince him that, with the help from his new higher power, he will be cured and able to go on in life like a normal person. Do not let him seek the truth of Christ. For as you know, if the Son does not set him free, then he will not be free indeed."

"Yes, sire," Nakot quickly responded, "I will be more subtle in my approach. I will influence him toward a false God, and if he gains some rewards in life, then he'll think he's on the right road."

"Good," replied Satan. "Do not allow him too much freedom though.

Remember, the boy has parents who are devoted to Christ, and they pray for him constantly. Continue using your strongest weapon, his addiction. If he does not seek Christ's salvation then you can manipulate him with the desire to stay high. Use that desire to strike a wedge between him and his family. You have to separate him from all who speak the truth."

"It is evident God has plans for the boy, so the only way to win this is to turn the boy against god. Start planting the thoughts in his mind that maybe there is something wrong with him. Maybe, there has always been something wrong with him. Why would God allow him to be born with this affliction? Does God possess a twisted sense of humor? Continue planting these thoughts in his mind until he said, 'Well, I won't serve a God like that.'"

Nakot stood in awe of the evil ingeniousness of Satan. "Wow, master. That must have been how you persuaded Eve."

Satan grinned, "Yes, it was something like that."

Nakot nodded, "I know I'll experience the same satisfaction with my case as you did with her."

"You better!" roared Satan as he departed like a bolt of lightning. Nakot sat alone outside the jail, formulating his battle plans while he waited for the next day to come.

The next day, the jail released me to Dana's custody. She had located a treatment facility in a town about seventy miles away. She had my bags packed when she picked me up from jail, and away we went. I didn't have insurance but was fortunate enough to have a grandmother willing to pay for the treatment. I spent the next thirty-five days trying to "find" myself and prepare for a sober life away from the security of the facility. I had developed a very unhealthy, deep resentment toward Dana because she didn't have to face the ridicule I got from both sides of our families. To everyone, she remained the innocent wife who was only trying to hold on to her husband, and I couldn't stand her for that.

I met a friend at an outside AA meeting that agreed to let me stay with him until I could get on my feet. I told Dana I couldn't return to Nowhere because there were too many bad memories and that I needed more time around people in recovery. The day I got out of treatment, Dana was there to pick me up. We traveled back to Nowhere so I could get my car and some more clothes. Dana was upset about my decision to stay with a friend but said she wanted to support me trying to stay sober.

I was only at the house about thirty minutes when I heard a knock on the back door. Dana was trying to get to the door before I could see who it was.

When she opened it, I rounded the corner just in time to see her trying to tell George it wasn't a good time for him to come by. George was another crack head who wanted to be a crack dealer. Apparently he and Dana had been smoking together—and who knows what else==the entire time I was away. When she closed the door, she saw me standing there and her face crumpled.

"Oh, Carl, I'm so sorry. I can't believe that he just showed up like that after all this time," she said as I turned to walk away. I knew better than to believe he just showed up out of the blue after staying away for over a month, but I didn't feel like listening to her lie to me, so I said nothing.

I grabbed my bags and walked out the door, saying, "You, see, this is why I can't come back here. There is no way I'll stay sober if the drugs keep coming to the house."

Dana was crying, but she made no attempt to stop me as I got in my car and drove away. Seeing George sparked an obsession in my mind. I had some money my family had sent to me, a car, and no lone looking over my shoulder. When I got to the highway, instead of turning right to go back to my friend's, I turned left and headed out to the bar. When I pulled into the lot, Scotty came running over. I told him I needed $100 worth, which he quickly gathered from a bag he had in his hand. I gave him another $5 for his pipe and quickly drove away. I spent the rest of the day driving back to my friend's house. He only lived seventy miles away, but I kept turning down dirt roads to smoke a rock, so it took me all day to get there. When the crack finally wore off, the remorse set in. I thought maybe I could just pretend it never happened, keep my original sobriety date, and keep going to 12-step meetings as if nothing was wrong. The thing about getting sober is, the only person you have to be totally honest with is yourself. I never went back to Nowhere. In fact, Dana and I soon separated.

FINDING PRISON

I MET A GIRL AT AN AA CONVENTION IN a small town in Mississippi. She had an impressive four years of sobriety under her belt. She was pretty, smart, sober, and someone I thought I needed in my life. We started seeing each other regularly, and it wasn't long before she got pregnant. I went from one marriage straight into another one. Because she was sober and a strong member of AA, I went to meetings with her on a regular basis. I didn't want to be sober; in fact, sobriety felt painful to me. But, I didn't want the problems that would arise between her and me if I started drinking again.

On my way to work one day, I stopped at a store for a cup of coffee. I was especially tired because I had worked very late the night before. When I was paying the cashier, I noticed several stacked bottles of something called Mini Thins. "What are these for?" I asked.

"They're like some kind of energy pills or something," he replied. I figured I'd give them a try, so I bought a bottle. In 1991, Mini Thins were nothing more than 25 mg of Ephedrine HCL (speed). I got into my car, popped the top, and took eight tablets. About thirty minutes later, I started feeling the effects. My scalp was tingling and my hands were shaking. I could feel my body temperature rise, along with my desire to clean something. I was happy to discover these pills, which I could buy legally, because they gave me a high very similar to that of methamphetamines. I took more of the pills each day. Before long, I was taking between seventy and ninety pills a day. I would have to take ten to twelve Unisom sleeping pills at night just to fall asleep.

This routine went on for about a year before I had to undergo knee surgery for an old football injury. With the knee surgery came a legitimate reason to take Hydrocodone. I hated taking the Mini Thins each day just to make it through.

After the surgery, I had six weeks in which I could just lay up and eat pain pills all day. Despite the pain, I thought I was in heaven. My tolerance level increased quickly, which meant I needed to devise a way to get more pills than the doctor was prescribing me; so I made prescriptions.

I won't go into the details about making prescriptions, because I don't want to give anyone any crazy ideas. Forging prescriptions is risky, even on a legitimate script pad, but forging them on home-made scripts is just plain stupid. I forged a lot of scripts at different pharmacies in Mississippi and Louisiana without any problems. The thing about getting away with illegal activities is that eventually you start getting sloppy.

One evening, I was at a Wal-Mart Pharmacy, presenting a forged script as I had done so many times before. The process seemed to be taking longer than normal, so I asked the girl behind the counter if there was a problem. She assured me there was no problem, that they were just a little backed up. I waited there another ten minutes or so before I got that gut feeling that something was wrong. Desperately wanting the pills, I went against my instincts to flee and decided to wait it out. After about thirty minutes of standing there, a man dressed in plain clothing tapped me on the shoulder. When I turned toward him, he presented a badge from inside his camouflaged jacket and asked me to step outside with him. When we got outside the store, he placed me under arrest and put me in the back of his unmarked detective's car. This was the first time I was arrested for forging prescriptions.

The girl I had married in Mississippi had a very influential family. Her brother was a judge, and he, along with the rest of her family, were well-respected members of the community. I mentioned his name during the interrogation, and lo and behold, I was set free that evening without having to go to jail. Shortly after that night, I decided to start drinking again, since it was the one thing I could do legally. This was like the straw that broke the camel's back for my sober wife.

She gave me an ultimatum; I had to choose either her and my daughter or the drugs and alcohol. I chose the drugs and alcohol. I convinced myself it wasn't about the drugs; it was that I wasn't going to be told what to do. I decided I was a grown man, and if I wanted to drink, then so be it. I left my family and moved to a city in central Louisiana called Alexandria. I was twenty-four years old in 1994, and for the first time since high school, I was unmarried. I went out to several bars and night-clubs on a regular basis. It didn't take long before I met several people whose interests were identical to mine—getting high.

Louisiana is a very festive state. There seemed to be a party going on somewhere in the state at all times. Raves (a large party with several DJs) popped up almost every weekend in New Orleans, Baton Rouge, or Lafayette. I and several buddies of mine became what were called "club kids." We bounced from rave to rave and night club to night club, taking large amounts of acid, ecstasy, and methamphetamines. We wore ridiculous clothing, crazy hats, and usually had an array of glow sticks to dance with.

I noticed the guys supplying the drugs seemed to be the most popular guys at the party, so I decided being a drug dealer was the way to go. I worked as a bartender at a fancy hotel at night and ran the roads in search of good products during the day. Despite what you may think or may have seen on TV, selling drugs is not just parties and having fun. The main reason I sold drugs was to supply my own needs without costing me any money. The problem with this kind of drug dealing is if I didn't sell the product quickly enough, I would start using it. I spent countless hours in search of good meth at decent prices so I could make a little money and still get high.

The most aggravating part of dealing meth was dealing with meth-heads. It's not uncommon to find a coke dealer that doesn't get high on cocaine. By not getting high on his supply, he can be more organized and less scandalous—in other words, a better dealer. With meth, everyone I bought it from got high off their own supply. Because meth keeps you up for days, you never know when a normally straight-up guy might be wigged out on a five-day bender. He would call to me he had some good stuff at a good price. I would always try it before I bought it, but sometimes what I would sample and what was in the bottom half of the bag were two different things. Drug-dealer policy is, if you buy it and leave with it, you bought it.

Because I didn't like selling stuff I knew was no good, I often ended up with a bunch o stuff I couldn't use or sell. Despite the aggravation, my need to shoot speed on a daily basis kept me in the game. One night, two friends and I decided to go to a club just south of Lafayette. We left Alexandria around midnight and headed south on a ninety-mile trip. One of the guys brought a half ounce of weed, and I brought a couple grams of speed.

Over the years, I have assisted several different cooks while they manufactured methamphetamines. The texture, smell, and appearance of the product changes depending on the chemicals used and the process of the manufacturing. One process generates a crystallized powder; the next can produce something that looks like small chards of broken glass. Users typically refer to the powder type as crystal-meth or crank. The glass-like stuff is called glass or ice. No matter what they call it, it's all homemade speed, classified as methamphetamines. Though I preferred to shoot speed, when I was around friends, I would only snort it. Smoking ice is the way most people do it today, but this was 1995, and we didn't know anything about smoking it at that time.

I kept my personal stash of speed in a vial, which I kept in a prescription pill bottle. Along with the vial, I kept a small piece of brass tubing to use as a straw for snorting the meth. The brass straw and the vial fit perfectly inside the pill bottle, and the bottle fit perfectly inside a small sealed compartment just below the stereo in my car.

We were about twenty miles from Lafayette when my buddy lit up a fat joint. I set the cruise control on seventy miles an hour, which was the speed limit.

Just after we finished the joint, we saw signs for an exit to get to Louisiana Downs Horse Race Track. There was a hill just before the exit, on which sat a sign dropping the speed limit from seventy to fifty-five. I noticed the signs as I passed them, but I didn't hit my brakes until I saw the cop sitting in the median.

As soon as I passed him, I looked in my rear-view mirror. My stomach dropped when I saw him turn on his lights and pull onto the highway behind me. I didn't want to look suspicious, so I pulled over immediately. When I got out of my car, I noticed not one but three cop cars had pulled up behind me. The first car was an unmarked detective's car, followed by two patrol cars, one of which was from the median. A uniformed officer exited each patrol car, and a detective in plain clothing exited the unmarked car.

The detective asked several time if he could search my car. I told him no three times before he decided to search it anyway. He found the dope, and, of course, I went to jail. It took almost a year in a legal battle before the charges were dropped. He didn't follow the correct procedure to search my car, so the judge suppressed the evidence, and I walked away clean.

My addiction to meth got worse. I couldn't keep a job in Alexandria, so I thought I'd try another geographical change. I moved back to Texas and took a job building houses. I was drinking heavily at night, and I started taking the Mini Thins each day. The Mini Thins had changed to a blend of 25mg of Ephedrine and a 200mg Guaifenesin. The Guaifenesin would make me nauseated, so I would often throw up after taking them. After a while, I was taking up to 120 pills a day. My body couldn't break down the pills well enough, so I would urinate a chalk-like substance for the first several hours after I took them. Between the painful chalk urine, the nausea, and the uncontrollable shakes that accompanied the pills, you would think I would stop. The truth is, I hated taking them every day. It was all I could do to swallow them without throwing up. I would lurch at the very thought of taking the pills. I guess my body was trying to tell me it didn't want that trash.

I hated taking them, but for some reason, I felt like I needed to be high to work properly. I felt like I needed some kind of speed to get through each day.

Of all the illegal drugs I've done, I'd say crack was always the easiest to find. I wasn't in Texas long before I found a couple of places to score crack. My routine became Mini Thins in the morning to go to work, crack in the afternoon, and a lot of beer and whiskey to drink myself to sleep at night. I followed this routine for months before I met a guy who was into meth. I immediately switched gears and started shooting meth again. I actually felt better about myself because I was no longer eating the pills or smoking crack. The meth and alcohol was all I needed. I would stay up for long periods of time, which caused me to get a little crazy. I stole from everyone, including family. I took a credit card from my uncle's house, thinking it belonged to my recently deceased grandfather. I bought TV's, tools, stereos—anything I could trade for dope.

After one month, and $4,500 later, I got a visit from my uncle. I vowed I would pay the money back if he wouldn't press charges. He agreed, but I never paid the money back. Besides my family, I was stealing from my employer. He figured it out and caught me one day trying to steal a VCR. I was so high on Adivan and alcohol, I passed out in my car with the VCR in the front seat. I woke up in jail with a theft charge. Because it was under $200, it was considered a Class A misdemeanor. The geographical cure of moving to Texas didn't work out. I bonded out of jail and moved back to Louisiana.

When I moved back to Alexandria, I hooked up with a guy I had known by reputation. He was known for always having coke and meth. He and I made runs to Dallas to score large amounts of meth. When we got back to Louisiana, I would sell it for him in exchange for a constant supply of dope and a place to stay. I began forging scripts again, and before long, I was again busted.

THE CHANGE

THE TRUTH IS, THESE CRAZY STORIES cold go on and on, but I'm afraid you'll grow tired and quit reading before I've made my point. I decided to tell part of my history so you will know that I know what it is to be a drug addict. I know what it is to be a slave to the desire to get high and never come down. I know what it is to give up my freedom, my wife, and my children to the power of chemicals.

I've been arrested a total of thirteen times. Nine of those times were with felony charges. Four of those nine ended in felony convictions. I've also been convicted of two Class A and two Class B misdemeanors. I've been to numerous county jails in Texas, Louisiana, and Mississippi and served two prison sentences in Texas. All in all, I've spent a little over three years of my life behind bars and ten years and probation. In addition to my probation and jail time, I've been to four residential treatment hospitals, one of which lasted for almost five months. I spent nine months in a state restitution center and six months in a halfway house. I did a six-month course of outpatient drug therapy. I've attended over a thousand different 12-stepmeetings.

I tried to commit suicide three times, overdosed three times, resulting in hospital stays, and survived two major life-threatening accidents. The first one was a horrific car accident, and the second, I severed the artery in my right arm. Both accidents occurred because I had been up for several days on meth, started drinking, and got sloppy. The car accident happened because I passed out while driving and smashed into a large pine tree. With my arm, I was trying to open a door to a rent house. It was a common back door with nine 6x9 panes of glass in the top half of the door. In my inebriated state, I missed the handle while trying to open it. My arm went through one of the panes of glass and severed the artery, just above the elbow of my right arm. It was a very-near-death experience, one I will never forget, but that wasn't enough to make me stop getting high.

It wasn't until I turned forty years old, during my second prison sentence, that I decided enough was enough. It was time for a change. For the first time, I was able to concede that maybe, just maybe, I wasn't smart enough to figure out how to fix me.

In the early years of my addiction I didn't think I had a problem with drugs. I truly believed I could manage them if I was careful. I just had to figure out how to stop getting caught. As the years progressed and the arrests kept happening, I started looking at myself in a different way. Each time I got locked up

I was running hard on whatever drug I was using at the time. In other words, if I was smoking crack, that was my drug of choice. So every time I got locked up, I would vow to stop using whatever drug I was running hard with at the time. I would think, *Well, I won't shoot dope anymore or smoke crack or forge scripts or whatever happened to land me in jail. I'll just do something harmless like drink beer.*

I now know what they told me in Narcotics Anonymous is absolutely true. *Thinking of alcohol as different from other drugs has caused a great many addicts to relapse. We cannot afford to be fooled by this. Alcohol is a drug.* Alcohol was always the catalyst for my quick return to the throws of hardware addiction.

Despite my absolute resolve, I was usually back at it within the first thirty days of my release.

Over the twenty-six years of my active addiction, my thought process changed. I went from believing I was in control to accepting that I had no control. For the last twelve years of my addiction I believed I had no choice but to be a drug addict. I convinced myself it wasn't my fault because I was born with a genetic flaw. I figured God was sadistic and when things were bad, I even cursed Him as if He was responsible for allowing me to be born that way.

It wasn't until 2009, while sitting in a prison cell in Jacksboro, Texas, that I opened my mind to hear from the Lord. I knew I was a few months away from getting out, so I prayed. My prayed was like this: "Well, God, I wouldn't blame you if you're not listening, or if you don't remember me at all. I haven't called on your name, except in the form of a curse word, for many years now. God, I wish you'd fix me. If you'll fix me then I'll serve you."

In other words, "If You'll do something, then I'll do something."

As I was praying, a voice in my head said, "Carl, I went to Calvary." So, I stopped to think about what that meant. All the stories I heard as a child came back to me. I remembered the story of Jesus, and I thought, *You know, Carl, Jesus is the Son of God. He came to earth just wanting to help everybody, and they beat him relentlessly, stripped him bare, and paraded him through the streets, kicking Him, laughing at Him, and spitting on Him in front of his own mother.* I tried to imagine what it must have felt like to have been in His shoes. I know when I really try to do something good for someone and they spit it back in my face, I get my feelings hurt and usually form a resentment. I can't imagine what the beatings must have felt like or how excruciating the pain must have been when they drove spikes through His wrists and feet. I tried to envision how humiliating it would be to be paraded through the streets like He was. I tried to imagine how much it would break my heart if those things were done to me by people I loved and was trying to help. When I stopped to think about how much Jesus must love us in order to go through with all that, it broke my heart.

As tears coursed down my cheeks, I prayed, "Lord, I am so sorry. Please forgive me."

It was then that I realized I had never truly been saved. I mean, I grew up in church, and at age fifteen, I stood in front of a church congregation and claimed to have been saved, but I did that for my own selfish gain. In that prison cell, I realized there had to be more to true Salvation than just muttering some words from a prayer. In that prison cell, I got a glimpse of Jesus and just how very real he is. At that point, I got down on one knee and humbly prayed for my salvation.

After praying that prayer and truly meaning it, I felt a sense of peace come over me unlike anything I have ever known. I noticed after praying that prayer, I developed a very real desire to learn more about my Savior. I picked up a New International Version Bible from the prison chaplain. It's a great study Bible, and I still have and use it today. One of the first things I read was Romans, 10:9-10:

> *That if you confess with your mouth, "Jesus is Lord," and believe in your heart that God raised him from the dead, you will be saved. For it is with your heart that you believe and are justified, and it is with your mouth that you confess and are saved.*

I probably heard that scripture read a hundred times over the years of going to church during my youth. I had confessed Jesus is Lord several times in the past, but it wasn't until I practiced the second part of the scripture that the real change began—when I believed whole heartedly that Jesus is real, that He is the Son of the one true living God, and that He endured that painful death for me. Then I knew above all else, I wanted to follow Him. I prayed, "Lord, I now know you are real, and I thank you for saving me, but what about this addiction I have? What about the temptations I'm going to have when I leave this prison and get back into the real world?"

In a very real voice in my mind, Jesus said to me, *"Carl, I hear your concerns and I understand. For you see, son, I too know what it is to be tempted. During my time on earth, in the form of man, I was subjected to temptation from Lucifer himself. Satan offered Me the world if I would deny God the Father and walk away from the cross. Despite the enormous amount of temptation, I stayed the course and completed My Father's will"*

I then realized Christ could have walked away from all of that. I can't even imagine how much temptation Jesus had to overcome in going to the cross. The temptations He had to overcome made my temptations seem minute and unworthy to compare. I realized if God doesn't do another thing for me, He's already done more than I could ever thank Him for. Over the next several months, I attended every church service that was available. I participated in Bible studies with other inmates, as well as reading and studying the Bible on myown.

I read a story about a man named Nicodemus. Nicodemus was a member of the Jewish high council during the time of Christ. To better illustrate this, I'll refer you to the Bible. In John 3:1-7, you'll read:

> *Now there was a man of Pharisees named Nicodemus, a member of the Jewish ruling council. He came to Jesus at night and said, "Rabbi, we know you are a teacher who has come from God. For no one could perform the miraculous signs you are doing if God were not with him." In reply Jesus declared, "I tell you the truth, no one can see the kingdom of God unless he is born again." "How can a man be born when he is old?" Nicodemus asked. "Surely he cannot enter a second time into his mother's womb to be born!" Jesus answered, "I tell you the truth, no one can enter the kingdom of God unless he is born of water and the Spirit. Flesh gives birth to flesh, but the Spirit gives birth to the Spirit. You should not be surprised at my saying, 'You must be born again.'"*

I knew to be saved meant the old me died and I was born again as a brand new creature in Christ. I no longer had to be the same old, pathetic junkie I was before. I started thinking a lot about the night

I'd seen what I would call a demon sitting on my bed laughing at me. I remembered a scripture from the Bible saying something about our daily struggle against unseen forces. I searched and found the scripture I was looking for. It's in the book of Ephesians, chapter 6, verse 12.

It states:

> *For our struggle is not against flesh and blood, but against the rulers, against the authorities, against the powers of this dark world and against the spiritual forces of evil in the heavenly realms.*

At the bottom of each page of the Study Bible was a breakdown of certain scriptures. For Ephesians 6:12, it states:

> *These who are not "flesh and blood" are demons over whom Satan has control. They are not mere fantasies—they are very real. We face a powerful army, whose goal is to defeat Christ's church. When we believe in Christ, these beings become our enemies, and they try every device to turn us away from him and back to sin.*

I read this with an open mind, and it all made sense. For the first time, I was able to see my addiction as more than a disease. In my addiction, I found it easier to convince myself that if it was a disease, then I had no choice; for some unknown reason, I was born afflicted.

I often said, "I didn't ask to be like this. I don't know why I can't stand being sober. It's like I can't stand being in my own skin. Why did I get this disease when so many others didn't?" that sounds a lot like, "why me, poor me," doesn't it? One of the first things we addicts learn is the art of self delusion. We become masters of self-pity, justification, and rationalization. We develop skills of manipulation, coercion, and acting. After thinking about that scripture, I was able to see myself being plagued by a bitter enemy—one that wants nothing more than to influence me into destroying my life and the lives of those around me.

In the penitentiary, I learned to never back down from a fight. If you back down from one fight, things will only get worse, and before long, someone will take advantage of your weakness. I never went looking for trouble, but I stood up when it came my way. My demon was just like that—an enemy coming to look for trouble. If I didn't make a stand against him, then things would only get worse. During the last few months of my prison sentence, I was able to start taking on the mindset that I am a brand new creature in Christ. I told the devil, "you know what, you're not getting any more of me. That's it, I'm done!" I was able to come out of prison a brand new man.

The day I left prison I was faced with an eight-hour bus ride home. This was not a prison bus, so I was under no observation. The bus made several stops at convenience stores that acted as bus depots. Upon our arrival at the first store, the enemy came at me hard. At first he tried to coerce me with the thought of how good a cold beer would taste and how much I deserved one as celebration for my release from prison. I quickly rejected that thought, so he came back even harder. A voice in my mind said, "Man, do you really think you're going to stay sober for the rest of your life? Do you realize how many times we've been at this crossroad? Come on now, what's the point? Let's just have a beer."

At that point I started to pray. I remembered Jesus rejected Satan three times before he fled. I also remembered reading in Luke a quote from Jesus. He said, "If any man wishes to be My disciple he must deny himself, take up his cross daily, and follow Me." I knew what I had to do. I called upon the power that Christ said is mine; the power that he shed His blood to give me. I commanded the enemy to flee and asked the Lord, "Father, what You have me do?"

For the remaining six-hour trip God filled my mind with the direction of this book. He gave me the title and layout of the story. As soon as I got home I went to work. I'm not a typist or what you'd call a book person. Actually I've only read a handful of books in my life, and they were read in prison. I wasn't real sure how to tell my story or if anyone would want to read it. I only knew I had a burning desire to tell everyone of the miraculous change Jesus Christ made in my life. It took me several months of writing to get this all on paper. Like I said, I'm not a typist.

After a few months of writing, I realized that a key part of my success in staying sober was my desire to help others. If you are a struggling addict or alcoholic, then your story may resemble parts of mine. I'm here to tell you the same transformation can take place in your life if you'll make a stand for God. Not based on what's in it for you, but because of what He's done for you.

First, you must be saved and born again. If you have never received the free gift of salvation, then I urge you to pray:

> *Lord Jesus, I humbly come before you as a lost child. I don't know how to get out of this miserable life I've been living, but I know You do. Lord, I ask You to please come into my life. I believe You to be my Lord and Savior. Please take me in and show me how to live. Please help me to be what You intended for me to be. I love You, Lord, and I thank You for loving me.*

If you pray that prayer and truly mean it, then you should feel confident that you are saved. Now, I'm not talking about just reciting the words and hoping it will get you out of some trouble. I'm talking about realizing you are talking to the Son of God. I'm talking about going to the Lord with proper respect and saying, "Lord, You don't have to do another thing for me. Thank You for what You have done for me. Now, what can I possibly do for You?" Brothers and sisters, I'm here to tell you, if you'll take on that type of mindset, your life will change for the better.

Up to this point, I've only talked about the rewards this transformation will give you in this physical lie. I haven't mentioned the best is yet to come. Once you're saved by grace, then you are guaranteed a spot in heaven with Christ and His church. To better illustrate, I'll refer you back to the Bible. In John 14, Jesus is telling the disciples that he must go away. He is referring to His upcoming death. He tells them that he is going to heaven to prepare a place for us. If you'll look at chapter 14, verses 1-7, you'll read:

> *Do not let your hearts be troubled. Trust in God, trust also in me. In my Father's house are many rooms; if it were not so, I would have told you. I am going there to prepare a place or you. And if I go and prepare a place for you, I will come back and take you to be with me that you also may be where I am. You know the way to the place where I am going." Thomas (one of the Disciples) said to him, "Lord we don't know where you are going, so how*

> *can we know the way?" Jesus answered,*
> *"I am the way, the truth, and the life. No*
> *one comes to the father except through*
> *me. If you really knew me, you would*
> *know my Father as well. From now on,*
> *you do know him and have seen him."*

You see, Jesus is the only answer. By being born again, the old me died. I am no longer some pathetic junkie spending enormous amounts of money trying to buy happiness. For twenty-six years I tried snorting it, smoking it, and shooting it, but I always ended up feeling worse once the high wore off. Today, I have joy. Joy because I'm not a slave to the devil and his chemicals. I genuinely feel good for the first time in my adult life. I am proud of myself, because I am finally becoming the man God intended for me to be. If you are a suffering addict or alcoholic, then I ask you, "When was the last time you felt proud of yourself?"

My brothers and sisters, I know how it is to feel hopeless. I know what it feels like to lose your friends, family, and self-respect. I also know what it is to be an overcomer. I know what it is to hold my head up proud despite my past. I know what it is to have peace, joy, love, and self-respect. All the good things I have in my life are because I chose to deny myself, take up my cross, and follow the Lord. I'm telling you, you too can have these things if you'll do the same. I've written this to tell you it's not too late to start over.

I can assure you, if you're a drug addict or alcoholic, then the first thing the devil's going to tempt you with is chemicals. If that doesn't work, then he'll come at you with your past. Oftentimes in our addiction, we burn all of our bridges, so our families and friends don't believe us when we say this is the last time. In all honesty, can you really blame them? It's going to take some work to regain trust from people who have known you. There are some people who will never trust you again. Do not let the enemy convince you that you cannot change. Satan wants you to think you've done too many bad things to ever be considered a winner. Nothing could be further from the truth. In fact, most everyone loves to hear a story where someone defied all the odds and came from behind to win the race.

Your life can be much like that race. All of the terrible things you might have done in your past can all be part of an amazing testimony. You see, God doesn't need your ability as much as your availability. If you'll trust in the Lord, make up your mind to stay sober, and get into a good church, God will open doors for you in ways you can't even imagine. When I say "get into a good church," I mean more than just going on an occasional Sunday. I mean get into a fellowship with other members of the church. I'm telling you that you alone can do this, but you cannot do this alone. We need support and fellowship with others who are striving for the same higher calling. If you're tired of losing everything, then I hope you'll try what I'm telling you.

A NEW BEGINNING

THE FINAL CHAPTER OF THIS STORY IS still being written because I'm still walking forward with our Lord. I'll tell you a little bit about where I am today and what I'm hoping to do. About a year and a half before I went to prison for the second time, I married a beautiful girl I had been with for eight years. Over the years of staying with me, this girl endured a lot, including my reluctance to make a marriage commitment. Because of the disastrous two marriages I'd had years ago, I vowed I would never again marry. I thank God that she stayed with me long enough to become my wife and see me as I am now.

Today, my wife and I have been married for a little over four years. We have a twelve-year-old daughter and a two-year-old son. My son was born while I was sitting in a Texas prison, four hundred miles from my home. I got locked up shortly after we found out she was pregnant. Considering the amount of meth I got caught with, I was very fortunate to receive a six-month sentence. I wasn't there for her entire pregnancy. I wasn't there to help her with the delivery of our son. I am very thankful she waited for me, but as you can imagine, she was pretty mad.

I am praying that my oldest daughter, the child from my second marriage will find it in her heart to forgive me for abandoning her so many years ago. It's like I said before—there are some people that will in time start to trust us, and there are those that will never trust us again.

In prison, I became friends with an inmate who led the praise and worship team before each church service. He was the son of a convicted felon. His son is the son of a convicted felon, and recently, his grandson became the son of a convicted felon. It occurred to me that if I didn't make a change, then it could easily be my children sitting in a prison one day. I now rejoice that my children will be awarded the same opportunity I was—to hear about Jesus. I can't stress to you how much I appreciate the fact that my parents made sure I heard all about the saving grace of Jesus Christ. As a child, I didn't appreciate having to go to church every Sunday morning and Wednesday night, but I'm sure glad I did. Once I had enough pain and heartache, I got alone in a prison cell and cried out to the Jesus that my mother taught me about. It was the same Jesus that replied, "All right, son, now get up and walk with Me. We have a lot of work to do."

My mother was the one person who never gave up on me. She was there every time I landed in Jail, treatment, or the emergency room. She would always tell me the same thing, "Son, you've got to have Jesus. Only He will make a difference in your life."

I would listen to her, but would think to myself, *Yeah right, mom. You have no idea what it's like to be an addict. There is no magical fix for me. I'll die this way, and that's just the way it is.*

Today, I can proudly tell you I know what she meant when she said, "Only He will make a difference in your life." My mother and I have a better relationship now than we have ever had. In fact, her inspiration flows through this story.

I've recently gone to visit my father. I have had little or no contact with him in over twenty years. No son wants to be embarrassed of himself in the eyes of his father, so I chose to stay away from mine. We are now in the process of redeveloping a relationship. For the first time I don't feel ashamed of my life. Praise God!

My wife and middle daughter cannot believe the miraculous change they see in me. For the first several months I was home, my wife kept waiting for me to change back into the person I was before. I kept telling her this time was different, that I was different, and finally, she started to believe me. My family and I attend worship services at Sagemont Church. I discovered this church two weeks after I got out of prison. As soon as I got out, I did reconnaissance on Sunday mornings in search of a church I could call home. The first church I went to was nice, but I didn't find the feeling I was looking for. The second Sunday, I walked into Sagemont. As soon as I walked in, I was greeted by an abundance of friendly faces saying, "Good morning!" "God bless you!" and "Welcome to Sagemont!" I found a seat in the back of the church and looked around at all the smiling, happy people. I could tell that for the most part, everyone I saw seemed to genuinely want to be there.

Even before the music started, I was getting a good vibe about this church. Once the music started, I knew I was onto something good. The second song was so moving, all I could do was bow my head and pray. The presence of God was so strong in there it overwhelmed me to the point I had tears flowing down my cheeks. The pastor came up and delivered a message with authority that Christ is the only answer, and that sealed the deal for me. I knew I had found a church home. Since then, I have become an active member of the church, and they are encouraging me and helping me get this story to you.

I am telling you these things in order to say this: If you are to the point that you're trying to figure out how to stay sober and continue walking on the road to victory, then you are going to need encouragement from others. If you don't find that in the first church you go to, then keep searching. Not all churches are created equal, and finding a good one is essential. If the message is not about Jesus Christ being the only true Savior, then you are in the wrong church. Keep searching until you find one that preaches the message of Christ. When you find a church that does that, then you'll find a congregation filled with people who want to help you. You see, a true born-again Christian wants nothing more than to encourage you and help you on your walk with our Lord.

If you read this story and just asked Jesus to be your Lord and Savior, then I should tell you this: The enemy is going to come at you now, possibly harder than ever. Satan still tries to catch me off guard with alluring temptations. He attaches those temptations to one of thousands of memories I have of getting high. The difference is, today, I can tell him, "No!" and it actually means something. The reason it means something is because I follow it with, "In the name of Jesus, get away from me Satan." I mean it when I say that; therefore, he has no choice but to flee. In addition to that statement, here are other instructions I follow: In the Bible in the book of Ephesians, the Apostle Paul tells us what we must do in order to stand against the enemy. Ephesians 6:13-17 states:

Therefore put on the full armor of God, so that when the day of evil comes, you may be able to stand your ground, and after you have done everything to stand. Stand firm then, with the belt of truth buckled around your waist, with the breastplate of righteousness in place, and your feet fitted with the readiness that comes from the gospel of peace. In addition to all of this take up the shield of faith, with which you can extinguish all the flaming arrows of the evil one. Take the helmet of salvation and the sword of the Spirit, which is the Word of God.

Now that you are saved, you should know that you have the full weight of God behind you. Know that when you put on the full armor of God, the enemy has no power of you unless you give it to him. Make up your mind to give the devil no more of your time, and move forward with helping others. I call it the 3-G effect: Get saved, Get up, Go forward. What I mean by helping others is to get involved with some sort of service work in your church. There are millions of suffering addicts and alcoholics out there who have tried for years to find a solution. If you have found the peace I have, then you know you have found the solution. I am asking you to join me in taking this fight to the enemy.

The fight I'm talking about is helping our brothers and sisters find salvation through Jesus Christ. By helping others out of the clutches of the evil one, we in essence slap him in the face. I warn you not to try this on your own. If Jesus is not the center of your motivation, then any attempt to battle with the devil will end in catastrophe. Put on the full armor of God and join me in helping others find their way out of the misery and into the light. Our military has a motto that in battle they never leave a man behind. I pray you'll join me in making this our motto.

A very wise lady made the following statement to me while we were having a cup of coffee. She said, "Carl, I firmly believe that if we are not going forward, then we'll go backwards." That simple statement made more sense to me than anything I had heard in years. I have used that statement to fuel me on several occasions. Many times while writing this story, the enemy tried to discourage me. He tried to tell me no one really cared to hear about my stupid little story and I was simply wasting my time in writing it. Several times, I almost started to believe him, but in a still, small voice, I heard, "Just keep writing, Carl."

What I've come to realize is that by trying to help others through writing this book, I've stayed sober. I don't even think about getting high anymore. In fact, the only way I could have written this story with such graphic details is because I asked the Lord to be with me each day before I started writing. In the past, if I even thought about shooting up, my stomach would turn and I would be filled with an unquenchable desire. I would go get high—every time, no matter what. Brothers and sisters, I'm here to tell you, God changes lives. God is no respecter of persons; what He has done for me, He will do for you. Now that you are a born-again believer, I pray you'll join me in telling others Jesus is the answer. Because of what Christ has done for me, I'm telling everybody. Won't you join me? I can assure you the rewards are worth it.

"Aahh, you stupid, stupid little man," screamed Nakot as he paced back and forth outside Carl's house. "Not only have I lost you, but now you're trying to shed light on our whole operation." Nakot stared at the ground in a sense of defeat as he asked himself, "How could this have happened?"

Just as that thought ended, Satan appeared. "How could this have happened, Nakot? I entrusted you with what should have been a simple task: Win me the soul of a lost drug addict. Now the boy's on a mission to expose us. I can't believe how badly you have failed me, you worthless piece of trash. I am sending you back to hell. You can start over again from the bottom. Although, I'm not sure you're qualified to handle a tormentor's position."

"What! No, sire," exclaimed Nakot. "I have been a successful tempter for decades now. It's not my fault you assigned me to one of those nightmare challenges. You know I deserve better than to be one of your tormenting foot soldiers."

"You deserve *nothing*!" roared Satan. "If there was a position less than a tormentor, that's where you would be. How many times have I heard you boast to Kansra saying, 'Oh, I've got him now, sire'? Well, you didn't get him, and just look at him now."

Nakot looked directly into Satan's eyes and said, "Well, Lucifer, you thought you had Christ when you put him in the grave, and look at Him now."

"*Rraahh!*" erupted from Satan's throat as he snatched up Nakot, tore him to pieces, and scattered his remains into the wind. Satan remained in the yard, breathing heavily for a moment before he appeared in the corner of Carl's bedroom. Carl was sitting on his bed proofreading his story while Jasos and Ditri stood guard.

"Bahh," barked Satan. "I guess you think this is funny?"

Jasos shook his head. "No Lucifer, we don't think anything about this war over the souls of God's creation is funny. But we do take great joy in seeing one of His creations become one of His children through the salvation of Christ."

Satan nodded his head. "Well, Christ might have his soul, but as long as that human is living on my earth, I will be there trying to destroy his life."

Ditri looked at Satan and calmly said, "That's why we'll be there with him as he grows on his walk with the Lord. God is pouring out His Spirit upon this man and preparing him to do great and mighty things. He has declared war upon you in the name of Jesus Christ, and God will equip him to carry Christ's message to the brokenhearted."

"Hah," Satan blurted out. "He's just one man who has spent most of his life working for me. What good can he possibly do for God's kingdom?"

Jasos stepped up and spoke with clear authority, saying, "King David was just one man. Moses was just one man. And Paul was just one man, who worked for you most of his life before God called him. Surely I don't have to remind you of what a difference they made for God's kingdom."

Ditri looked down at Carl fondly. "They were ordinary men who heard God's call and obeyed His Will. God has not changed, Lucifer. You above all should know that. The same God that called upon them still calls upon men today. Kansra was right when he said that few listen and take action, but for the few that do, great and mighty things await them."

Satan paused for a moment as he stood there taking in what Ditri said before he looked up and said, "Well, you give it your best shot, and you can bet I'll be giving it mine. We'll see how it all works out. I'll see you two another day on this battlefield."

Satan was about to leave when he turned back and said, "Oh yeah, before I go, there's one more thing I must know. Twenty-two years ago, in that boy's bedroom, his soul should have been mine to claim. One of my former soldiers said he thought the boy was able to see him. Did he?"

Ditri looked at Jasos as Jasos nodded.

"Why?" Satan asked as his expression went from puzzled to alarmed. "To tell this tale, of course."

Satan lowered his face but never took his stare off Ditri and Jasos. Smoke boiled from his nostrils as he began to hiss and growl—as if his actions would frighten the two angels.

Jasos looked at Ditri as if to say, "Really?" A white, hot light glowed about Ditri as he raised his right arm toward heaven and with great authority said, "In the name of Jesus Christ, Son of the one true living God, I command you, Lucifer, to leave this place." Before Ditri could finish the command, Satan disappeared in a clap of thunder.

Ditri turned his gaze toward Carl and said, "Well, he seems to be heading in the right direction."

Jasos approvingly nodded his head. "Yes, I believe you're right. He seems to really have taken hold of the belief that if God is with him, then nothing can stand against him. I know as long as he remains focused on the Lord and continues trying to help others find victory through salvation, he'll continue growing stronger and stronger."

Ditri nodded solemnly. "I'm thankful that we'll have the opportunity to walk with him on this new and exciting journey."

Jasos smiled. "Yeah, Ditri, me too."

AFTERWORD

THE STORY YOU JUST READ IS A COMBI-nation of actual events from my life blended with what some would call fiction. I word it like that because it is not what I would call fiction. The Bible has numerous passages in it about angels and demons, but for some reason, modern man has labeled them as fictitious characters.

Twenty-two years ago, in a bedroom of my father's home, I did see the terrifying creature I chose to call Nakot. I believe that creature was a very real demon sitting on my bed laughing at me. I believe I was very near to a fatal overdose, and God allowed me to see into the spiritual realm. I believe I was allowed to do that to better illustrate this story. I did not see the other characters in this story, but I do believe there is a very real spiritual war going on all around us, all the time.

A story like this leaves a lot of room for skepticism if you read it with a closed mind. I pray you will be open-minded to these questions: What if there's more to addiction than a mental or genetic disease that randomly afflicts different people? What if there is a spiritual battle taking place right now for your very soul? No matter if you're an addict, alcoholic, or neither, the enemy wants to destroy your life. I know the sooner we figure that out and take hold of the hand of our Savior, the better our lives become. I can't even begin to put into words how much better my life has become now that I no longer try to fight my battles on my own.

I can't stress how much I would love to talk to you. I pray you found this story encouraging and are ready to move forward. If you would like to talk to me about anything involving your walk with our Lord, please contact me, Carl Miller, at The Men of Sagemont Ministry @

> Sagemont Church
> 11300 S Sam Houston Pkwy E
> Houston, TX 77089-4699
> (281) 481-8770